Stephen Greenleaf Bulfinch

Honor

The Slave-Dealer's Daughter

Stephen Greenleaf Bulfinch

Honor

The Slave-Dealer's Daughter

ISBN/EAN: 9783744713603

Printed in Europe, USA, Canada, Australia, Japan

Cover: Foto ©ninafisch / pixelio.de

More available books at **www.hansebooks.com**

HONOR;

or,

THE SLAVE-DEALER'S DAUGHTER.

BY

STEPHEN G. BULFINCH.

"I could not love thee, dear, so much,
Loved I not honor more."
COLONEL RICHARD LOVELACE. 1642.

BOSTON:
WILLIAM V. SPENCER,
134 WASHINGTON STREET.
1864.

Entered, according to Act of Congress, in the year 1863, by
STEPHEN G. BULFINCH,
In the Clerk's Office of the District Court of the District of Massachusetts.

ELECTROTYPED AT THE
Boston Stereotype Foundry,
No. 4 Spring Lane.

PREFACE.

IN introducing this little story to the public, the author would observe that while the tale, as a whole, is fictitious, the sketches of southern scenery, life, and manners, are derived from a residence of many years in that section of our country.

He has wished to do justice to the better side of southern character, while portraying some features of that fatal system, which has been scarce less injurious to the master than to the slave, and has now consummated its work of evil by the crimes and the horrors of the present rebellion, — to find therein, let us hope, its own destruction.

Some particulars in the narrative, which may seem improbable, are derived from fact; such is the incident connected with a popular song; and such the singular legal decisions referred to in the charge of Judge Stanley to the jury.

CONTENTS.

CHAPTER		PAGE
I.	"A Trap to catch a Sunbeam."	7
II.	"What's in a Name?"	15
III.	An Arrival and a Scene.	21
IV.	"He left his Country for his Country's Good."	30
V.	Coming to the Point.	37
VI.	The Slave-Dealer.	47
VII.	Temptation.	55
VIII.	Travelling south.	66
IX.	Life in Xenophon.	73
X.	A Stage-Coach and its Passengers.	83
XI.	Tusculum.	92
XII.	The Evil every where.	103
XIII.	The Gold Region.	111
XIV.	Hasty and Incautious.	118
XV.	The Tavern and its Inmates.	125
XVI.	A Strange Scruple.	135
XVII.	The Mob.	149
XVIII.	Country Living and Religion.	163
XIX.	An Indian Chief and a Stray Poet.	176
XX.	Into the Lion's Mouth.	191
XXI.	The Trial.	204
XXII.	The Defence.	215
XXIII.	The Unexpected Witness.	221
XXIV.	The Conclusion.	230

1*

HONOR;

OR,

THE SLAVE-DEALER'S DAUGHTER.

CHAPTER I.

"A TRAP TO CATCH A SUNBEAM."

THE town of Irvine, forty or fifty years ago, wore a different aspect from what it does at present: for the cotton factory did not then exist; there were not half as many houses; and French roofs and bay windows had not made their appearance. The ground now occupied by the railroad station, from which you look down on the factory buildings around the stream, and on the village rising up the hill beyond, was then part of Captain Bates's farm. But there were the hills around; there was Mount Josey, with its blue dome terminating the vista up the valley. There, too, was the stream; and though not as laborious as at present, it did something besides singing, for it turned a mill. The mill-pond spread out where it spreads now, except that then its border of pond lilies was farther down. The building of the new dam has raised the water, and almost drowned out the willows there to the left of the old Livingston house, that substantial square mansion, rather low-studded, whose grounds are separated from the rest of the village by the road that crosses the bridge.

That Livingston house used to be a pretty place; some might think, prettier than it is now; for its grounds have been encroached on in other directions than that of the pond, though what is left of them has been very much improved. The elms in front, now so large, were handsome trees even then; there was not that arbor-vitæ hedge, but there were more lilacs. Mr. Livingston was much interested in his apples and pears, which were splendid fruit, and still more so in his peach-trees, which — ungrateful things! — would yield, for all his care, poor specimens compared with those of New Jersey.

Mrs. Livingston was quite as much interested in her flower-garden. Besides her fondness for flowers, it gave her something to take care of, and supplied thus in a degree the one want of her life.

It was a peaceful house, — sometimes a little too peaceful. The Livingstons would have been better pleased if the silence of their home had been broken by infant voices; but though married for several years, the blessing of children had not been granted to them; and, except when young nephews and nieces came to visit them, the stillness of the house was more deep than suited the kind-hearted pair. Formed, both of them, to find pleasure in conferring it, they needed an object towards which their hearts could expand themselves, — one whom they could care for, provide for, feel for, and pray for, — in whom they could treasure up hopes and expectations, which, even if they never should be realized, would at least have conferred a blessing in the prospect.

Mr. Livingston was a lawyer, who had retired from business with more than enough for his own wants; and nowhere did the minister, Dr. Solesby, find a more ready attention paid to his representations, where the distresses of the poor were the theme, and any thing could be done for their relief. Such a case once occurred, which formed a memorable epoch in the family history.

"Mrs. Livingston," said Dr. Solesby, "I have called to ask if you could come with me to see that poor woman at Bailey's tavern." The preparations were soon made, and the lady and her clerical friend were on their way. They passed out of the quiet street of dwelling-houses and gardens, and entered that which was the scene of business in the little town. Passing the various stores, they stopped at the piazza entrance of the hotel. There were but few people about, and those in the bar-room; so, without stopping to speak to any, Dr. Solesby led the way through the entry and up the stairs to an attic in the back part of the house, where, through his interest in their behalf, the family in question had been allowed to remain.

The room was uncarpeted, and the two chairs, bed, and table, were of the simplest kind. A woman was lying on the bed; and a little girl, about five years old, was seated near her on a stool.

"How kind of your reverence to come so soon again!" said the woman, when he had saluted her by the name of Mrs. Witham. "And of this lady, too," she added, casting a glance around, and uttering a word of excuse for the appearance of her room.

"Never mind that," said Mrs. Livingston. "I am sorry to see you so ill, — and sorry that I did not know of it before. How long have you been in Irvine?"

"About five months, ma'am," said the woman. "I came here with my husband, who was in search of work at his trade; but there seemed little for him to do here; and after staying a month, he left me, to try and find a place for himself, and promised to let me know, that I might join him."

"Have you not heard from him since?" inquired the lady.

"No, ma'am. He is no great writer, and he wouldn't care to write, unless he had some good news to tell. And there's no knowing how far he's gone. I shouldn't wonder if he had gone to New O'leens; for he often talked about it."

"But how could he find money to take the journey, when he left you in such a situation?"

"That's just it, ma'am," said Mrs. Witham. He had money enough when he went away; for he had sold the shop and our furniture when we left Eastford. That was the place we settled in first, when we came from England; but he took a dislike to it, because they didn't treat him kindly. They told stories on him, and said that he was a drunken Englishman, and that he stole. But, as I was saying, that's just why I am so poor off, because John said he'd have to take the money, to go round and look out a place where he could work. He left me a dollar, and I meant to find a little place and take in washing; but I took sick, and should have died before now, if the good minister hadn't looked up friends for me."

"You tire yourself," said Mrs. Livingston, kindly; "do not talk any more now. Here," said she to the little girl, "are you mother's nurse, little one?"

"I take care of mammy a little," said the child, timidly.

"Don't you wish that father would come back, so as to take care of her better?" said the clergyman.

The child cast down her eyes, and murmured a "yes, sir;" the tone of which seemed to belie its meaning.

"Betsy don't like her father as she ought to," said the woman. "I suppose it's because he whips her sometimes more than he ought to do; but that's because he's in liquor, you know, ma'am; and he can't help what he does then. But you're a naughty girl, Betsy, not to love your father, and the lady won't like you, if you do so."

The child turned her tearful eyes up to Mrs. Livingston, and said, with a mixture of feeling and sullenness, "I don't like anybody but mother."

"But you won't have no mother much longer," said the woman, "and then you must mind what father says, when he comes back. O, I wish John would come back, if he was ever so sharp with Betsy or with me. But now he's gone to New O'leens, and I shall never see him again; and what will become of Betsy?"

"Trust your child to Him who is the Father of the fatherless," said the minister.

The woman looked at him uncertainly for a minute, and then said, "I know what you mean, sir, but I ain't good enough to trust like that. As bad as John is sometimes to me, he'd see that his child shouldn't starve. O, I wish John was back!"

"My friend," said Mrs. Livingston, who found a purpose which her husband and herself had indefinitely cherished, brought to active life by the sweet looks and unprotected condition of the child, "you have cause to trust in God, for he has already provided friends for you and yours. If this sickness of yours should be to death, I will take care of your child."

The woman looked up with a grateful smile; but at

once another expression, an eager and a deprecating one, came upon her face; and she answered, "But what would John do, if he came home, and found Betsy given away? He must have her, ma'am, whether or no, if he comes back and wants her; and I'm sure he will want her if he lives to come back."

"But how can you speak for him," said Mrs. Livingston, with more warmth than consideration, "when he has abused you and your child through intemperance, and at last abandoned you?"

"O," said the woman, "as for drinking, many's the good man that's not himself when he's taken his drop of comfort; and as for his leaving me, why, of course it is to find work, so that he may take care of us all. But John's a good husband when he's himself, ma'am; and he'll be a good father to Betsy, when he comes back some day. And if you'll keep her till then, ma'am, and see that she's clothed and fed, I'm sure God will reward you; but the child must be John's, when John wants her."

The illness of Mrs. Witham, notwithstanding the kind care of her new friend, increased, and terminated with her death. The offer made by Mrs. Livingston was willingly confirmed by her husband; and after the humble funeral was over, Dr. Solesby directed the carriage which alone had followed the hearse, to be driven to Mr. Livingston's, and, descending himself, handed from it Mrs.

Livingston and the little girl, who was now clothed in deep mourning. As they walked up the pathway, Mr. Livingston advanced from the door, and, taking the little one in his arms, gave a father's kiss and a father's blessing to his *adopted child.*

CHAPTER II.

"WHAT'S IN A NAME?"

THE Livingstons, in adopting little Betsy Witham, had been somewhat disquieted by the earnest reservation which the mother had made in favor of the father's rights, provided he should return. They thought best to make inquiries, however, in the village of Eastford, from which the Withams had come; and in this Dr. Solesby was able to assist them, by corresponding with a minister in that vicinity, with whom he was acquainted. From this friend he learned that the Withams were, as the woman had intimated, English people — that they had lived in Eastford about three years, little Betsy being about two years old at the time of their arrival. The father, it appeared, was a carpenter, and an expert workman, when he chose to work; but he was not only addicted to dissipation, but his character lay under the suspicion of darker offences. When sober, he was reserved and sullen; when excited by drink, noisy and quarrelsome. A number of petty offences against property had been committed while they lived in Eastford. Hen-roosts and gardens, which had previously, in that quiet town, been as safe as the gold in a bank vault, and possibly safer, were mysteriously plundered; and people said that the drunken carpenter's family lived well, as far as poultry and fruit went. The man, too, in his cups, had incautiously boasted of his exploits, in "the old country," in the poaching line; and, when some surprise was expressed, had defended his actions by a logic which would apply as well to Yankee farm-yards as to English preserves. Still, positive proof was wanting, and none liked to be prominent in seeking it, because some were held in awe by the strength and violent character of the man, and others pitied his feeble and suffering wife. At last, however, a house in a town near Eastford was entered in the night; silver spoons, a watch, and some other articles, and seventy dollars in money, were missing; and suspicion fell on Witham too strongly for the matter to be kept in silence. He was arrested, but denied the charge made against him, and demanded that his house should be searched. This was done in the most thorough manner; but none of the stolen property was found, nor did any circumstance come to light which could confirm the suspicion that had been entertained. The carpenter complained bitterly of the unfriendliness of the people, and declared his determination to remove from the neighborhood, where, as he said, he had been persecuted. It was not long before the real thief was discovered, and Witham freed from all suspicion of the robbery. He continued in his purpose, however, saying sullenly that he would not stay where he had been so treated. The sale of his goods at auction was well attended, and the family left the village, not much to the regret of its inhabitants, with the means thus obtained.

Such was the account which Dr. Solesby received from his friend, the Rev. Mr. Wilson. To this he could add, of his own knowledge, that the family, on arriving at Irvine, had taken a room at the hotel; that Mrs. Witham's feeble health had lapsed into serious illness, which her husband seemed to regard with much more of vexation than of sympathy; that at length Witham had left his wife, avowedly to consult an English physician in the county town; and that from his journey he had never returned. The woman, when the time appointed for his return passed by, seemed less surprised than afflicted; and when it was found that Witham had gone without paying his bill, and had left no money for that purpose with his wife, the conclusion was clear, that it was on his side an intended flight. The tavern-keeper was disposed to lay blame upon the woman also; but compassion and Dr. Solesby's intercession prevailed; and the poor woman was allowed to spend her last days in the humble room where she was found by Mrs. Livingston.

The account which has just been given was the subject

of long and anxious consultation between Mr. and Mrs. Livingston and the worthy minister. Where had Witham gone? Would he return? Would he desire to claim his child? Could he take it, without their consent, from those who had assumed the charge of it when deserted by him? Mr. Livingston studied his law-books, and consulted his neighbor and professional brother, Mr. Richards; but as neither of them could foretell whether the father would return soon or late, able or unable to maintain the child, with a steady character, or a worthless vagabond, little satisfaction could be obtained.

One thing was plain — the child was to be taken care of; and this duty and privilege of the present time Mr. and Mrs. Livingston determined to accept, leaving to the future the decision of other questions. So, when the little Betsy was brought to their house, she was received on an uncertain footing in theory, but, as it quickly appeared, a very definite one in practice. They intended to be very cautious, but the child's winning ways got the better of their caution. Their hearts became warmer and warmer towards the little orphan, and before a month was out she was the orphan Betsy no longer, but Elizabeth, or, by contraction, Lizzie, the beloved daughter of Mr. and Mrs. Livingston. How the change came about may be imagined, in its other stages, from what passed in regard to the names by which the little charge should salute her new guardians.

"I think," said Mr. Livingston, after some conversation on this point, "that I must give up to you. 'Mr. Livingston' and 'Mrs. Livingston' would be rather formal, I admit. Pity the name is such a long one!"

"But 'aunt' and 'uncle,'" said his wife.

"Yes, 'aunt' and 'uncle' will do. That is affectionate; and though I don't like confounding the relations of life, yet this is an excepted case. 'Aunt' and 'uncle' let it be."

With this decision they met little Lizzie in the breakfast room, where she had gone before them. The child left the kitten, with which she had been playing, and nestling to her protector's breast, began to give an account of pussy's tricks.

"And, mother," said she, "kitty was trying to catch hold of the table-cloth, and Bridget drove her away, for fear she would pull the teapot over. Do you think, mother, kitty could pull over that big teapot?"

Mrs. Livingston knew that she ought to tell her to call her 'aunt'; but the words would not come. That name 'mother' was so sweet to her ears, that she could not check the child for using it. Mr. Livingston saw his wife's weakness, and determined to show his strength.

"Come here, Lizzie," said he; "I have something to say to you."

"Let me go, mother; I must go to father," said the little one; and she ran laughing to him, and seated herself upon his knee.

"You call me 'father,' dear," began Mr. Livingston, not quite as strong as he had intended to be.

"O, yes; I've got a nice, dear father," said the child. "All little girls have fathers and mothers, that they live with."

"But Mrs. Witham was your real mother, my dear," said the cautious protector.

"Yes," said Lizzie, with a shade of sadness for an instant; and then added, "When I staid over there, she was my mother; and now you are my mother, and you are my father. All little girls have fathers and mothers."

"What can she know about it, husband?" said his wife; "let her call us so; it will do no harm."

"But, Lizzie," continued he, not so ready to relinquish his point, "if your real father, Mr. Witham, comes back, you know you must ——"

"O, I don't want to go back! I don't want to go back!" cried the little girl, in an agony of fear; "for father scolds and whips me so; and now he'll do it worse than ever, because mother isn't there to say 'Please don't.' O, I want to stay with you, and have you for father and mother."

"Call us 'uncle' and 'aunt,'" said Mr. Livingston.

"Father and mother," said the child, pleadingly; "all little girls have fathers and mothers."

And so the question was practically settled.

CHAPTER III.

AN ARRIVAL, AND A SCENE.

THUS Betsy Witham was changed into Lizzie Livingston. The surname indeed was scarcely thought of, till Miss Brown's bill was presented, "for one quarter's tuition of Miss Livingston;" whereon, after some conversation, it was decided, that though it was a mistake on the part of Miss Brown, it would not be worth while to say any thing to her about it. So successive bills were paid, in which the same error regularly occurred; all the school associates of Lizzie fell into the same misapprehension. Lizzie herself regarded Livingston as her name, and even her protectors forgot that there was any mistake in the matter. So passed three years, during which the little girl met and overcame the difficulties of learning, from the a, b, c, to the multiplication table, and proved herself a bright, intelligent, and affectionate child.

One day, when Lizzie was engaged in her studies at school, a man presented himself at the door, and inquired for Betsy Witham. The name was a strange one to the scholar who had answered his knock, and with some impatience he asked to see the teacher. Miss Brown accordingly left the class which she was hearing, and with dignified step advanced to the door. The man who stood there was not in appearance such as she was used to converse with; for hers was a private school, patronized by the wealthier people of the village, by some from aristocratic feeling, by others from parental tenderness or caution, in view of the hardships and exposures which they dreaded for their children in the public schools. The visitor was rather showily than well dressed, with hat jantily disposed on one side, and that arrangement of stock, vest, and watch-chain, which marks the effort at gentility that defeats itself. The man's face might have been handsome, but that it bore the marks of intemperate habits and unregulated passion.

"Is there a little girl here of the name of Betsy Witham?" said the man to Miss Brown.

"No, sir," replied the lady; "I have no scholar of that name."

"I think you have, ma'am," said the man, bluntly. "I was told she came to school here, and had for some years. My name is Witham; I am her father, and I insist upon seeing her."

Miss Brown's answer had been given in forgetfulness of the story of her pupil, Lizzie Livingston, and the former name of the little girl had never been impressed on her memory. But now that story recurred to her mind.

"I am not sure, sir," she replied, "that I was right in my first answer. There is a little girl here who goes by a different name, but who may be your daughter. Was she not adopted by Mr. Livingston?"

"Goes by a different name!" said the man. "I wonder what right any one has to give another name to my child. That's the one, ma'am, and I want to see her, about the quickest; and I'd like to see any body that would take upon him to keep father and child apart."

The voice of the father was loud enough to be heard through the thin partition which separated the entry from the school-room. Lizzie heard it without a thought that she was concerned in the discussion which appeared to be so angrily carried on by one of the parties. But she raised her eyes, as others did, when the teacher reëntered, received with some surprise her signal to come forward, and was ushered into the entry with no idea why she was sent for.

"This is the little girl, sir," said Miss Brown. Witham gazed upon her with surprise and pleasure.

"I should not have known you, little one," said he; "and of course you don't know me. I am your father, dear, and I've come home, pretty well off in the world, to take you to live with me. So, put on your bonnet, and show me the place where you live; for I must go and see the folks there, and thank them for taking care of you. I don't mean to steal you away. I've no need to, for you're my daughter, and nobody has a right to keep you from me."

Lizzie stood in bewildered astonishment. She had long ceased to think of any earthly father but Mr. Livingston; and the remembrances of early childhood, as they came to her again, were not such as to make her overjoyed at the sight of her real parent. The teacher, however, thought it her duty to interfere.

" Mr. Witham," said she, " I think it would be better for you to call on Mr. Livingston without the little girl.- I have nothing to say against your claim to her as her father, but that is not for me to settle. It was Mr. and Mrs. Livingston who left her in my charge, and I am answerable to them."

" You think, ma'am, I'll steal her away? Why, don't you see I have no occasion. I'm the child's own father, and Mr. Lewiston, or whatever his name is, can't come between me and her. Come, Betsy, put on your things, and let's go and see these friends of yours."

The child, bewildered as she was, and not much pleased with the paternal claim, caught with some hope at the idea suggested by his use of a name which had now become strange to her.

" My name isn't Betsy," said she ; " it is Lizzie Livingston."

" Livingston," said the man with an oath. " Don't say that to me again, unless you want me to knock you down. If you've forgotten your own name and your father's looks, I guess you have not forgotten the feeling of his right hand. Come along this minute, you silly slut," as the frightened child began to cry.

"Mr. Witham," said the lady, with firmness, "I cannot allow you to take the child at present. I have only your own word for it that you are her father, and, as I said before, I am accountable to Mr. Livingston."

This name brought forth another profane exclamation. "Come along," said the father, fiercely; and as the girl hung back, and pressed to her teacher, he seized her, and shaking her violently, gave her a blow upon the face.

All was now confusion. The children, who had before listened in mute curiosity and fear to Witham's loud and angry voice, now excited by Lizzie's cries, rushed into the entry; and while some of the older ones gathered round and tried to soothe her, the younger ones fled, bonnetless, towards their homes. Lizzie was crying as if her heart would break. The teacher, who had stood a moment in silent indignation, now seeing her suffering pupil in friendly hands, turned, with no little severity in her manner, to Witham.

"You see, sir, what your violence has done. You take but a poor way to make your child love you, or to induce her present protectors to relinquish her. For one, I assure you that not only you shall not take her from my school, but that I will not suffer her to go home, except under sufficient guard."

"We'll see about that," said the man, who, though shamed at first by the excitement caused through his violence, was roused again by Miss Brown's tone of defiance. He pushed aside one of the girls, who was trying to comfort Lizzie, and seizing the child in his arms, began to carry her from the school-house.

Nearly opposite was the office of lawyer Richards — a neat one-story building, within the same enclosure with the lawyer's mansion, and overshadowed by the same elms. The squire was at this time absent; and perhaps it was in consequence of this that his nephew, Fred Bryant, who sat at a green-covered table near one of the front windows, had suffered his eyes to wander from his Greek Grammar sufficiently to notice the visit of the stranger at Miss Brown's. After the man had entered, Fred returned to the adjective that was before him; but having partly committed it to memory, he thought it as well not to look at the book, but repeated its declension over to himself, while steadily gazing out of the window. At Lizzie's cry the boy dropped his adjective, and rose from his seat; and when Witham came out, bearing the child, and followed by the whole terrified school, Fred rushed from the office, and was across the street in a moment.

"What are you doing, you scoundrel?" he cried. "Put that child down! Help, help! Mr. Williams! Mr. Johnson!" he cried, as some of the storekeepers appeared at their doors. "Here's a man carrying off a little girl, and she's crying! Why, it's Lizzie Livingston," he added, as he caught sight of the child's face. This discovery kindled his blood still more, and with another command to put the child down, the boy of fourteen grappled with the powerful and reckless man.

Witham, though encumbered with the child, shook off and threw down his young assailant; but Johnson, Williams, and others, came running up.

"What is this about?" "What are you doing with that child?" "For shame, for shame!" exclaimed one and another.

"Don't touch him, my lad," said Mr. Johnson, the storekeeper, as the boy rose, and seemed about to recommence the unequal contest. "We'll see justice done. You're a brave boy, but you're no match for a man."

"What is all this?" said Dr. Solesby, whose house was near, and who, though a man of peace, was yet not the man to hold back when the innocent and feeble were to be protected.

Others came round, some from their houses, — to which their frightened children had carried the tidings, — some from passing in the street; and there were loud and indignant voices at the outrage which had been committed.

The voices subsided suddenly, however, when Witham declared himself the father of the child. The man saw his advantage, and pressed it, conquering his passion, by a strong effort, sufficiently for his present purpose.

"I am the child's own father," he said, "and she is the only one I have. I'm a poor man; and while I've been gone, my wife died, and Squire Somebody has took my child, and dizened her out, and made her forget her own name. But all that don't prevent her from being my child still. If I've got angry and struck her, I've had some reason; and a father has a right to correct his children. You've none of you any right to stop me, and stop me you shall not. Make way there, and let's see if Yankees will see child and father separated." Lizzie, having ceased her screams and abandoned resistance, lay motionless in his arms.

"He has the best right, of course, to his own child," said Johnson.

"It may be a question for the lawyers," said Williams, the shoemaker, "but I won't interfere to take a girl from her own father."

"But when her own father goes off and leaves her to perish," said young Brooks, the carpenter, "it is hard if he can come back and take her all the same as if he had been the best of parents—take her away, too, from those who had provided for her when he had deserted her."

"But I guess Squire Richards would tell you, Brooks," said Johnson, "that a father's a father, any how."

Dr. Solesby now interposed. "Mr. Witham," said he, "I was with your wife at the time she died, and it certainly was her wish that you should have your child. I am sure my friend Mr. Livingston will do what is right in the matter. There is no need of taking her away in this forcible manner. And it is rather hard, when he and his wife have treated her so kindly for years, after you had desert — I mean, when you were not here to take care of her yourself — that she should be snatched from them as if they had stolen her. Look," he added; "the poor child is half dead with fright. Bring her into my house, close by here, and let her have a little time to recover. Depend upon it, no harm shall be done to your rights in the matter."

The father looked at his little girl, and found that she had indeed fainted. He was not altogether sorry for this excuse to accept the temporary compromise offered him by the minister; for it had by this time occurred to him that the charge of a child, who for the present must be in some sort a prisoner, would be no slight care. To the minister's house, therefore, he bore his insensible burden, and left her in the charge of Mrs. Solesby, after receiving her husband's solemn assurance that Lizzie should not leave the house until the following day.

CHAPTER IV.

"HE LEFT HIS COUNTRY FOR HIS COUNTRY'S GOOD."

JOHN WITHAM was the son of an English farmer, the tenant of a small farm on the estate of Lord Cloudesley. In spite of an early reputation for wild daring, or perhaps even assisted by that reputation, the handsome youth found favor in the eyes of Betsy Jennings, the daughter of a neighboring tenant. They married young; and the child who bore her mother's name was the youngest of three, the two elder having died in those scenes of fatigue and privation to which their father's vices had exposed them. For strong drink, which was used by all around him, was to Witham not merely a temptation to excess in its own use, — it excited his imagination and kindled his passions. As he came more and more under its power, and within the circle of companions to which it conducted him, his days were less given to his business as a carpenter, and his nights more to poaching in the preserves of Cloudesley Manor. His offences of this description were for some time suspected; and, had not the steward, a cousin of Witham's wife, been willingly blind for her sake, the suspicions might have been readily confirmed. At last, however, the young man's reputation became so bad, and his acts so impossible to be overlooked, that a sudden emigration to America was the only alternative to a prison. The carpenter's cottage was found closed one morning, long after the wife was usually astir, and the officers of justice, who had been employed by the steward, arrived only to learn from an idle boy that Witham and his family had been seen, the evening before, going towards the "Cloudesley Arms," at a time which indicated that they would take the night coach for Liverpool. The steward, who had accompanied the officers, seemed greatly disappointed and indignant. He urged an immediate pursuit, and only with apparent reluctance suffered himself to be persuaded that it would be more than the arrest of a poacher was worth, to track him through the wilderness of a great city; and that if the country was rid of him, it was as well that he should leave it at his own expense, as to be sent to a penal colony at the public cost. None knew better than the steward, however, where the money came from for this sudden flight; for he had himself advanced it from funds of Lord Cloudesley in his hands, on a pledge of repayment from his uncle, the father of Mrs. Witham.

The absconding carpenter found his way to the New World; but he brought his Old-World habits with him. His course from the time of his landing till he abandoned his wife to the compassion of the good people of Irvine, has been already briefly indicated. The fact was, the fancy of the wild and unprincipled man had been fired by the accounts he heard from persons recently returned from the South and South-West. In a new country, not yet subjected to the control of law, he felt certain of that success which he was determined to gain either by the exercise of his trade, or, if that failed, by shorter and darker paths. In the years he spent there, he narrowly escaped, in several instances, being shot in private quarrel, or hung by Lynch law; he had tried a variety of callings, nearly corresponding to the nursery summary, "carpenter, sailor, soldier, gentleman, butcher, thief;" and returned, at last, with means enough to establish him in business in an older section of the country, and determined to reclaim the wife and child whom he had deserted.

He was somewhat shocked to find that the wife who so patiently endured his evil ways, had sunk so soon beneath the trials which separation from him she loved had made harder to bear. He had not expected this; but, counting on the sympathy and aid which he found were in this country so freely extended to those in poverty, he had supposed that she would be taken care of, while his own course would not be impeded by the presence of a sick wife and a young child. Towards those who had taken charge of his daughter, his mind wavered between gratitude for their kindness and jealousy of their influence.

He determined to see her and to reclaim her. Yet, as in returning he had expected to find his wife and child together, he was unprepared with any plan for the care and education of his daughter. As, after the scene at the school-house, he thought over this matter at the hotel, his reflections took a form more favorable than before to the continuance of the child with her present protectors.

"I wonder," said he to himself, "what sort of people these Livingstons are. Proud enough, I'll be sworn. But they've dressed up Betsy neat, and taken care of her, when she was nothing to them. They shall not keep her from me, however. And yet, if I take her, what can I do with her? Here I have no place fixed on to live in, and I don't care to settle down any where quite yet. A little girl like her wants some woman to take care of her — some decent woman, too; and who? Poor Betsy! Well, that's over; but I don't feel like marrying just now."

The result of a night spent in reflections like these, was, that on the following day Witham repaired to Dr. Solesby's with a disposition more conciliatory than he had previously shown. He accompanied the minister to Mr. Livingston's, and met that gentleman and his wife with some words in excuse of his violence the day before, thanked them for the care they had taken of his daughter, and expressed his willingness that she should remain with them for the present. The Livingstons were anxious to obtain from him an entire surrender of the child whom they now habitually regarded as their own. They urged their claim upon Lizzie, founded on her abandonment by her father. This excited Witham's resentment, and the conference threatened to have an angry ending; but Dr. Solesby acting as peacemaker, the matter was settled at last by a compromise, or rather an indefinite postponement. Witham saw his daughter, and endeavored by caresses to remove the unpleasant impression of the school-house scene. The Livingstons heard at length, with great satisfaction, that their visitor intended to leave the village on the following day. He gave little account of his plans, further than that he should go to New York, and look about him for a while; that by and by he intended to settle down, and that then he should want Betsy to come and live with him.

The Livingstons were careful neither to commit themselves by assenting to this, nor to excite him by contradicting it; and they saw him depart at last with a feeling of relief for the present, but of dread for the future. They had become strongly attached to their little charge, and felt that without her their house would be desolate indeed. But their anxiety to retain her was not on their own account alone. They shrunk from seeing her in the absolute power of one so ill fitted either to guide or govern her, as the father whose parting from her had been in base desertion, and whose return was in abuse and violence. But at least a respite was given. Unable to penetrate the future, they withdrew their minds from painful, and, as it seemed to them, useless anticipation; and as months again passed on without intelligence of Witham, they ceased to speak of him; and cherished their adopted darling, with the increasing hope that she would be theirs while their life should last, and render to their old age the offices of filial affection.

And years passed on, and still Lizzie shared the home of those who loved her as their own child. A few visits, made by her father without previous notice, reminded her of his existence, and awakened more of fear than of love, and more of curiosity than of fear. Her guardians thought it right that as soon as she reached a suitable age, she should have full information of the early circumstances of her own life; and this she received in part from Mrs. Livingston, and in part from Dr. Solesby. It was with deep emotion that she heard repeated her mother's earnest charge that she should not be kept from her father, if he ever returned to claim her. As other years passed on, the thought of that possible claim, and of the difficulties and the duties that might result from it, became blended with other thoughts, the effect in part of temperament, and in part of education. Naturally imaginative, she read eagerly those works of fiction, and especially of poetry, which the judgment of her guardians allowed for her perusal; and she loved in leisure moments to muse upon the incidents there described, and to fancy how she would have acted under the circumstances in which some favorite heroine was placed. This tendency might have led to unhealthy dreaminess, had not Mrs. Livingston instilled, with the utmost care, the sentiments of religious and moral obligation, and accustomed her, in every time of doubt, to ask of herself the question, What is right? Thus romance and poetry took their place, in the development of her mind, in harmony with the more serious teaching she received. Her enthusiastic character fixed its aspirations on the pure and the true; on virtue, honor, usefulness, self-sacrifice. Her favorite heroines were the Siberian exile, who made her way across the deserts to obtain her father's pardon; the Scotch girl, who with similar exertion saved the sister whom she would not save by falsehood; and the daughter of Wallenstein, who taught her lover to prefer honor and duty to herself and her father's cause. Thus, too, for herself she dreamed at times of a self-sacrificing future; and especially when saddened, as she sometimes was, at the thought that she might be called to leave her pleasant home and her beloved guardians, she would turn for comfort to the imaginations of duties opening else where. She would fancy a distant but not unpleasant home, to which she might add what would otherwise be wanting of attractiveness, and where her patience might calm her father's passionate feelings, her persuasions check his tendency to any wrong self-indulgence, and her love soothe his declining days. Meantime she busied herself in constant gentle efforts for those around her, in the happy home of the present.

CHAPTER V.

COMING TO THE POINT.

THE boy Frederick Bryant meantime was ripening into a young man. With the lively fancies suited to his age, mingled thoughts of improvement, honor, usefulness, and a gentle presence seemed to float through all his visions, the gay and the grave alike. Often, often in the autumn, after their acquaintance began, had he watched from his uncle's office door till Lizzie appeared, and followed her with his eyes along the street under the trees, until she turned in at the door of the school-house. At such times he would fancy what deeds he would perform, if that rude man should appear and offer any injury to the little girl; then, when he had lost sight of her, he would turn to his baize-covered table in the corner of the office, and try his pen in writing, in different hands, the name of Lizzie Livingston, until Mr. Richards's entrance suggested the expediency of a return to his Virgil.

Since those days he had passed through his college course with honor, and had now commenced the study of law, in the office of an eminent counsellor in Boston. He was, therefore, only an occasional visitant at Irvine; and when he returned there, as the time drew nigh for his admission to the bar, he looked with deeper interest than ever on the child of former years, and observed with delight the change that had taken place in her, more marked than any between his previous visits. Nor was she less pleased with her boy-protector, in his transformation into a tall and gentlemanly young lawyer. The intercourse between them was at first a little constrained, neither being quite sure of their mutual position. But very quickly the old familiarity returned, and, if they did not play together as noisily as in former days, there was not less enjoyment in their renewed acquaintance. Music was a favorite art with them both, and Lizzie's voice and Frederick's suited each other well; or his fine execution on the flute afforded an admirable accompaniment to hers on the piano. Without a thought in the mind of either, that looked beyond the present, their meetings gave life a different aspect to them both. The Livingstons, more keen-sighted, were in no doubt to what the intimacy tended, but saw no reason to discourage it; for Frederick Bryant stood high for character and promise; and, if they felt pained at the thought of Lizzie's leaving their home, even for that of a husband, it still seemed that an early engagement would afford some security against the possible capricious interference of her father.

It was on an afternoon in the latter part of summer, that Frederick and Lizzie had been with a party of friends to a sail upon the pond, — still known by its Indian name of Sunkesuck, — about a mile west of Irvine village. They now strolled homeward, in company with Henry Waldron, James Finch, and Mary Merton. Mary was a year or two older than Lizzie, and very conscious of the difference. Waldron was her devoted, but apparently not favored admirer; while Finch was one of those young men who enjoy the society of all ladies, but seem resolved to be made captive by none. Mary had been conversing with both the gentlemen, taking care not to show a preference to either, until, in passing a brook on stepping-stones, she was obliged, in taking the support of one, to reject that of the other. Waldron advanced first, and, stepping on the first of the stones, offered his hand to Mary.

"O, I am afraid," said she, drawing back. "Let me rest a moment, for I should slip if I went on now. Go on, Mr. Waldron; do not wait for me: Mr. Finch, don't let me detain you. I'll stay for the others."

Waldron, discouraged, went on; Finch followed more slowly, when Bryant and Lizzie, who had been conversing a few steps in the rear, came up, and, without noticing the purpose of Miss Merton's delay, passed on, Frederick supporting Lizzie carefully across the brook. Miss Merton looked vexed, and Finch laughed and returned.

"That is civility," said she, "to leave me here and go

on with that school girl. How perfectly blind the man is! He can see nothing but little A, B, C."

"Cupid is blind," said Finch. "Miss Merton, shall we cross the brook?" And he assisted her across, meeting half way poor Waldron, who was returning to offer again his rejected aid.

Waldron turned now disconsolately away. But the coquette had no mind to discourage him too far. "Look at Fred Bryant and that little girl, Mr. Waldron," said she. "What do you suppose he is talking about?"

"Something tender, I fancy," said Waldron.

"Tender! Nonsense! He's examining her in geography or spelling. Is not Fred a member of the school committee?"

"The poor things are so engaged, they'll lose their way," said Finch. "Waldron, can't you go forward and take care of them?"

"I might as well be the one too many there as here," said the indignant lover; and, going forward at a rapid walk, he passed the couple in front, only saying, in a low voice, as he did so, "Don't court too openly, Fred."

Frederick looked back, and stopped till the two in the rear came up, the coquette covering her disappointment at Waldron's withdrawal by a laugh. She and her remaining escort turned at length into a road which conducted to her father's house. Bryant, to whom Waldron's words had furnished the key of his own feelings, had suddenly become silent.

Lizzie had not heard the remark, but she knew Mary well enough to understand Waldron's sudden flight.

"There," said she, "Mary Merton has been tormenting poor Waldron again, and he has gone off in indignation. How can she take pleasure in making him unhappy!"

"You would not do so, Lizzie, would you?"

"I hope not — but I can't tell. The temptation has never come to me, and 'tis doubtful whether it will when I am grown up."

"But, if it did, I am sure, Lizzie, sure, that your heart is too good to trifle with the feelings of one who loves you."

His tone was very earnest, and Lizzie felt an excitement she did not understand; yet, true to one of her principles, to defend the absent, she replied, —

"Perhaps Mr. Waldron misunderstood her. Indeed, his extreme devotion is so obvious that it furnishes a provocation, almost an excuse, for a little coquetry."

"'O, wad some power the giftie gie us
To see oursels as ithers see us!'"

replied Bryant. He was thinking of Waldron's warning to him, and coupling it with this remark upon the giver of the warning.

Lizzie looked up surprised. "Does my sentiment shock you, Frederick?" said she. "I would be the last to defend real, intentional coquetry; but I hope poor Mary is really not guilty of that."

"Whether so or not, I am sure, dear girl, you never could be."

What further passed during that walk — which proved longer than the distance home required — we do not know; but Lizzie and Mrs. Livingston had a long talk that night, and Mr. Bryant came to see Mr. Livingston the next day. The young man declared in warm terms his attachment to Lizzie, spoke with modest confidence of his own prospects in business, and asked Mr. Livingston to permit their engagement. They were both young, he knew, and he would not ask that their marriage should at once take place, but he urged his wishes to be received as an approved suitor.

Mr. Livingston was surprised, as many a parent has been, to find that his little girl had become in the eyes of others a woman. He had approved the growing intimacy, but had not expected it to ripen quite so soon. At first, he was disposed to laugh the offer aside, on account of the youth of the parties; but this would not do. The young friend who sat before him, as full of serious purpose as of warm attachment, was unquestionably a man; and if he still thought of Lizzie as a child, he must admit that her childish years were passing rapidly away; and when they should be over, who so fit to make her happy as this same youth?

Bryant's parents, now no more, Mr. Livingston had known and respected highly; their son appeared to inherit the character of his father, as well as the resemblance, which, at that moment, seemed to his father's friend stronger than ever.

The expenses of an education had indeed nearly exhausted the orphan's slender patrimony; but with the patronage of his uncle Richards, and his own abilities, there seemed no danger but that he could find adequate support; and to whom should Mr. Livingston's own property descend, but to his adopted daughter?

Such thoughts passed through the good man's mind as he sat thoughtful and silent, scarce hearing the earnest pleading of his visitor; but the last of them recalled an objection which appeared insurmountable.

"My dear young friend," he said, "I do not know to whom I should give my consent more readily, if Lizzie is willing to give hers; but, you remember, I am not really her father."

"But her father leaves her entirely to you," said the young man. "He has hardly ever come to see her; and, from what I remember of him, I should suppose his visits could not be much desired. What right would he have, after neglecting her all her life, to interfere with objections to a marriage which you should approve? My blood boils now, when I think of the brutal way he treated her when she was a little child."

"Why, Fred, you were her champion so long ago as that," said Mr. Livingston, with a smile. "Perhaps Mr. Witham might like it still less, to find her not only engaged, but engaged to the boy that undertook to fight him in her behalf."

"He ought not to bear malice, for I got the worst of it," said Frederick. "But really, dear sir, this man's character is a reason in itself for our engagement. Who can protect her so well as a husband?"

"But you do not propose an immediate marriage?"

"No, I did not; but, now I think of it, under these circumstances, with this man's claim hanging over her all the time, would it not be better to give me at once the legal title, that would enable me to hold her against all the world?"

"Too fast, too fast, my earnest young lover. How would it seem on my part, when the poor man came back, and found that I had married off his daughter at sixteen, without giving him notice? Lizzie would never consent to it, either; and it would not seem like you to steal a march, and avail yourself of the father's absence in such a way as that."

Frederick blushed, and excused himself with some confusion. "But," said he, recovering himself, "if we ought not to be married, can we not be engaged? If her father returns, he can make inquiries about me. I trust," he added, proudly, "he will hear nothing that will give him just grounds to break off the engagement."

"No, my dear fellow; an engagement ought not to be formed under such circumstances. It would be wrong towards Witham, and would be laying up trouble for yourself and Lizzie, and all of us."

"But then, sir, can we not find this man, and induce

him to give his consent? Have you no information where he is, that we could write to him, or that I could go and see him?"

"None, whatever. He comes unexpectedly, and leaves no word where he is going. Indeed, I must confess, I have wished to have as little to do with him as possible. I have treated him decently when he came; and when he left, I have been glad of it, and have let him go without wishing to know where. Perhaps I ought not to have yielded to a feeling of aversion; but I have had some reason besides. If he should commit some desperate action, and be in danger from the law, it would be quite as well that I should not know where he was to be found."

"It is too bad that Lizzie's fate should depend on such a man! But if he can be found, sir, have I your consent that I should try to obtain his? And, until he is found, may I come and see Lizzie as formerly?"

"It cannot be quite as formerly, Frederick. You and Lizzie cannot be much in each other's society, after what has passed, without its going further than I can now in honor permit. I cannot forbid you the house, both as a friend yourself, and as the son of an old friend; but you ought not to come as Lizzie's lover, and you would not like to come as a stranger."

"I don't see, then, but that I am in effect forbidden," said the young man, rising.

"No, my dear boy, do not be angry. I will do the

best I can. Visit us occasionally; I will try all means I can think of to discover Witham; and, if he is found, I trust all will be well. At any rate, when Lizzie is of age, her father's consent will no longer be required by law or honor; and I do not think we need wait for any other consideration."

Young Bryant thanked his friend, though rather sadly, and returned slowly to his room at his uncle Richards's.

CHAPTER VI.

THE SLAVE-DEALER.

SINCE the conversation recorded in our last chapter, Mr. Bryant had been absent for a time; had been examined and admitted to the bar; had returned, and placed his sign below that of his uncle on the office in Irvine. The interest taken by the Livingston family in these events had removed whatever feeling of constraint had arisen between them and their young friend; and their intercourse was again on its old familiar footing, when an event took place which the young man had earnestly desired. This was the return of Mr. Witham.

He came in showy vest, with brilliant watch-guard and unfailing cigar. He came not alone. In a bold, scrawling hand, he entered on the hotel register the names of "Mr. and Mrs. Witham." The latter person was a woman of feeble and timid aspect, several years younger than her husband, and who had evidently been married long enough to know the strength of her husband's will, and to submit to it entirely.

Witham called upon the Livingstons with his wife, and made the latter acquainted with his daughter. Lizzie and her new mother met each other with looks of mutual fear. Witham observed it, and exclaimed with a laugh, "Why, I don't know which seems the most frightened. Cheer up, Betsy; there's nothing to be afraid of in Susan — your mother, I mean. She's only a sight too easy — hasn't got spirit enough to manage a kitten. And, Susan, I'll warrant you'll find Betsy a good girl." The two looked at each other, and the detection by each of a feeling like her own, produced a mutual smile, and a mutual disposition to be friends.

Still, it was with a sort of shudder that Lizzie heard from her father that he had come to claim her at last. He had been successful in the South-West, — in what business he did not say, — had married there, and had now come back to New England with the purpose of returning in the autumn, and establishing himself as keeper of a hotel. His daughter was to go with him; he spoke of this not as a subject of consultation, but as something decided upon. He thanked Mr. and Mrs. Livingston for their care of her; and, as he spoke, a feeling of the real extent of his obligation to them seemed to come upon him, perhaps for the first time; for it was with much warmth that he repeated his thanks, and declared that he should never forget how they had taken charge of his poor girl when there was no one else to stand by her, and had brought her up to look like a lady.

Mr. and Mrs. Livingston were not a little embarrassed. They could not deny the general right of a father to the services of his child under age; and Witham's circumstances in life, and even his manners, were so far improved, that it was difficult to state the precise grounds why he should be considered-unfit to take charge of his own daughter. The man's appearance was not prepossessing, and the prospect of his home at a hotel in Alabama was any thing but agreeable to the northern feelings of Lizzie's friends. They both felt deeply the loss they should sustain, the desolation of their own house when the child who had so long been its light was taken from it; but even this feeling was overpowered in that of anxiety for her.

Mrs. Livingston inquired as to the size and character of the town in which Witham intended to reside.

"It's a fine place, ma'am, for that country; its name's Xenophon, the county town of Saunders County. The great things they deals in round there is cotton and niggers; so there's white and black, the two extremes to choose between."

"Have you many negroes about you, Mr. Witham?" said Mrs. Livingston.

"O, plenty — rather more than plenty — so many they're in each other's way. Betsy won't have a thing to do but sit in the parlor and thrum the piano, except she may have to take her mother's place sometimes, looking after those lazy blackeys. About them, the traders stops pretty often with a good sight of 'em, coming from Virginia; but they won't be in Betsy's way."

"You have negro-traders stopping at the house, father?" said Lizzie. "It seems to me I should be afraid of the very sight of such a man."

"It wouldn't be a worse sight than you have seen, Betsy; and I can tell you, the money that comes from negro-trading is mighty convenient."

The inference which might have been drawn as to Witham's own history was prevented by the entrance of Frederick Bryant, who was introduced by Mr. Livingston to Lizzie's father and mother. Witham, however, after this interruption, resumed his former subject in a loud tone.

"You don't think much of nigger-traders round here, I reckon; but I can tell you, at the South they are as fine gentlemen as any. Some of the great planters and some squeamish city folks do turn up their noses at us, — that is, at the traders; but I don't know any of them but will come and buy a nigger for all that, when they want one; and I don't know as it's any worse to sell than it is to buy."

"So our abolitionists say, Mr. Witham," said Bryant. "They say the system is all one; if one part is right, all is right, and if one part is wrong, all is wrong. If the slave trade is wrong, it is wrong to hold slaves; the receiver is as bad as the thief."

"Thief's rather a hard name for a man that's had his slaves grow up on his own plantation. But I know what you mean, and I think so far the *abolutionists* is about right,—that if one part's bad, all's bad, and if one part's good, all's good. Now, I say, it's right to hold slaves; it's right to buy 'em, it's right to sell 'em; it's right to bring 'em from Virginia, and it's right to bring 'em from Africa; and I don't care what any Yankee [we omit the oath] says to the contrary."

The party looked at each other a moment in silence. Fred, whose indignation was held in check by a strong wish to conciliate Lizzie's father, tried to change the subject by mentioning the news of the day. But the effort was not a successful one, for that news suggested a conversation on the political questions then agitating the country; and on these the visitor again displayed offensively the arrogant dogmatism of ignorance and self-interest. Fred saw that he had made no progress; and, too honest to conceal his real opinions, he found it his best course to withdraw, leaving his intended suit to Mr. Witham to be urged at a more favorable time.

The next day Frederick saw Witham in private, and made an offer of his hand to Lizzie, referring her father to Mr. Livingston and Mr. Richards for a further knowledge of his character and prospects. But the negro-trader had been so little pleased with the young man the day before, that he received the proposal very coldly. He only answered at first that Betsy was too young, and that he wanted her to be with him now, as he had not had her with him for so many years. Frederick repressed the impatient answer which sought utterance, that the affection which had waited so long might wait longer, and besought the privilege of an engagement, or at least permission to correspond. But Witham did not choose to have a son-in-law whose deportment and principles were a reproach to his own. "Besides," thought he to himself, "there is no need of throwing her away upon a Yankee lawyer. She's a fine-looking girl, and there are smart young fellows enough in Xenophon, or, if not there, in Montgomery, or, if not there, in New Orleans, that will be glad to make her mistress of their land and niggers." So the interview between the suitor and the father ended with a blunt refusal on the part of the latter, and with high wrath indifferently concealed on the part of the former.

Fred, however, was not to be so baffled. He conversed with Mrs. Livingston, and found her in deep distress at the anticipated loss of her adopted child — a loss embittered by the evidence which every hour's intercourse with Witham increased, — of his want of cultivation, his narrow and sordid mind, and his looseness of principle. From her the young lawyer resorted to his uncle, and inquired of him with earnestness whether the law would sanction the claim of Witham to resume his child, against her own will, and that of the friends who had cherished her as their own, and had borne the entire expense of her education. Mr. Richards assented to the weight of the considerations thus named, but suggested those which balanced them. Witham had never surrendered his claim over his child; that claim had been acknowledged by the Livingstons not only by implication but expressly; and whatever the decision might be, Mr. Richards pointed out to his nephew the painful character, in every respect, of an appeal to law on such a subject; the agony of the choice to which the young lady would be subjected, obliged to take a part against either her real or her adopting father; and the misery of having her name and the names of her friends spread before the public, with every detail that impertinent curiosity could collect, in the papers of the day. There was but one claim, Mr. Richards said, which superseded that of a father; and that was a husband's.

"O that I had that claim!" said the young man. "And if Lizzie would consent to let me rescue her from this living death, this banishment to Alabama, this living among slaves and slave-drivers, it might be done."

"How would you manage about the marriage license?" said his uncle, smiling. "You would not have a runaway match, and go to New Hampshire? That would not do for you, a Sunday school teacher at Dr. Solesby's church."

And so saying, the good lawyer went forth to attend to some business at the Registry of Deeds, little thinking that he had suggested to his nephew to commit a deed, which, though palliated by circumstances, would be registered against him by the feelings of the community, and by the plain laws of natural and of Christian rectitude.

CHAPTER VII.

TEMPTATION.

WITHAM and his wife remained in Irvine for a time. Their accommodations at the hotel were very different from those which had been unwillingly bestowed upon the dying mother. The English carpenter, now appearing as a "gentleman from the South," insisted on the best apartments and the best fare that the house afforded. He was loud and important in the bar-room; and it was with some difficulty that the tavern-keeper contrived to conceal his guest's potations behind the thin veil of decency which increasing excitement on the subject of temperance rendered needful. Witham rode out frequently, driving the most spirited horses that could be procured. Sometimes his wife accompanied him; sometimes he called at the Livingstons', and took his daughter; and sometimes he had the company of a weak youth named Pickett, who boarded at the hotel, and in whose eyes the stranger was a glorious object, from the show he made, and his taste in brandy and in horses. Once, in a moment of good nature, he asked Fred to go with him; but the young man, more honest than prudent, replied to the showy slave-trader with so ill a grace, that Witham swore deeper than ever that he would never let that proud puppy come near Betsy.

At length he left the town, to attend, as he said, to some business in New York; and Mrs. Witham remained at the hotel till his return. The Livingstons, who had seen his course with increasing dislike, breathed freer in his absence; and Lizzie, as she stood at the private door of the hotel, almost blamed herself for not feeling that sinking of the heart which she had experienced there, when expecting to meet her father.

She found her step-mother in a room, such as hotel parlors are apt to be, stiffly fine, with much of show, but little of comfort. Two books lay on the centre-table, the one a quarto volume full of coarse portraits of eminent persons, alternating with pages full of advertisements; and the other a Bible, bearing on its substantial covers the inscription, "Presented to the Tenadnuck House, Irvine, by the Washington County Bible Society." Tenadnuck, it may be observed by the way, was the name which a learned professor had declared to be the true Indian designation of the neighboring mountain; and the endeavor was strongly made, but as yet with imperfect success, to bring it into common use, instead of the homely appellation of Mount Josey.

Mrs. Witham was sitting in a rocking-chair, with her

face turned from the window, slowly rocking, and gazing at the empty grate. She looked up with a smile of pleasure, yet with something of embarrassment, as her stepdaughter entered, and said, —

"Well, Miss Betsy, I'm glad to see you."

"I thought you might be lonely, ma'am, since Mr. Witham — I mean since father — is gone," replied Lizzie.

"Why, yes," said the elder female. "I am lonesome, rather. But it isn't because John is gone, for he often goes away, and leaves me a long time together; but this house seems so strange and so grand-like, I can't get used to it. I didn't mind it when he was here; but now I don't like to go about alone, and it's so queer calling on these white people to help one. When I'm to home, I don't mind calling on the niggers when I want any thing; but these white servants ——. How a white man can make a nigger of hisself, and be ordered about, I don't see."

"I have seen so few black people, I should feel strange in speaking to one."

"Why, law, I don't feel strange about that at all. They ain't like us, no way, — to be spoke to as if we was on our p's and q's with 'em. They mind right easy; and I tell you they've got to mind, too, when John's about. He'll make 'em stand round, the roughest of 'em."

"Does father own many slaves?" said Lizzie, timidly.

"O, sometimes many, and sometimes none at all," said

the wife. "It's just as happens; but commonly about November the yard's pretty full; and then in the winter they go off, except some bad bargains, that stay along till spring."

The daughter looked at her step-mother with a bewildered expression. "The yard!" she repeated. "Do they stay out in the yard?"

"O, when I say the yard, I mean the places that's built in it — the jail, and the nigger-houses, and all."

"Jail!" said Lizzie. "Excuse me, I know it is rude to repeat your words, but I don't understand. What has my father to do with a jail?"

"O, law!" said Mrs. Witham, laughing. "That's the place where he shuts up the new niggers, or any that's just going to be sold. Didn't you know, Miss Betsy," she added, "that your father was a slave-dealer?"

"My father a slave-dealer!" repeated the girl with a voice of dismay.

"Yes, he's a slave-trader, and a very good business it is. He's made money at it, hand over hand. He went into it first with my brother, who had been in the business before; and that's the way I come to know him."

"But what a horrid business," said Lizzie, "to buy and sell human beings! I can't bear to think of my father engaged in such a work!"

"Why, miss, you needn't be a looking down on your father for what he does," said his helpmeet, with some anger in her voice. "And it doesn't seem very polite either, for all you're so well eddicated, to talk so about a trade that my husband and my brother is in. But don't cry, Betsy. It must seem strange to you, I suppose; but there's no harm in it. Old father Williamson, the Methodist preacher, often says God made the race of Ham to be slaves, and it's right they should be. And if it's right to buy and sell them, why, then, the men that deal in 'em is just like any other merchants."

"But does father treat them kindly?"

"O, yes; as kindly as any body. They have to be whipped sometimes, you know; but he takes care not to overwork them, nor nothing. You see they wouldn't sell so well. Sometimes he's rough; but then," her voice sinking, and a tear in her eye, "sometimes he's pretty rough with me."

"But the separating of husband and wife ——"

"Why, dear, it isn't his fault. If a planter comes and sells him a likely gal, how is he to know she's got a husband? Most likely she hasn't, but only some one that lived with her. And then he does what he can to get her a husband soon. But you ain't going, Miss Betsy, be you?"

"Yes," said Lizzie, rising. "Please to excuse me now, and forgive me for my rudeness. It was all so new to me; but I hope I shall learn to bear it."

The unhappy girl returned to the pleasant home, which soon was to be hers no longer. With difficulty had she schooled her mind, — not indeed to submit, for that was at once resolved on, — but to submit without an expression of the deep repugnance that she felt at going to a distant, unknown section with such a father as hers appeared to be. But then she had supposed him a merchant, engaged in some honorable branch of business. Now she had learned that he was a slave-dealer — a man who had enriched himself by trafficking in the flesh and blood of his fellow-creatures — a man whose vocation was despised even by those who employed him, whether to relieve them of troublesome slaves, or to furnish their fields with new laborers. Happily, her ideas of the revolting character of the business were indefinite. The horrors before her were in great part unknown; and, when she had reached her home, and relieved her feelings in solitary tears, she sought and found strength for duty. As she rose from her knees, she said aloud, "Come what may, I will be a faithful daughter."

When Lizzie appeared at the evening meal, the friends who had watched her for some weeks with saddened hearts had no suspicion that the day had been one of peculiar mental trial. The dejection which they had detected through her studious effort to conceal it seemed to have gone. Her manner was more natural; and if they missed the careless gayety of the child, they had in its place something, unknown before, of the dignity of the woman. So completely had the high thought that occupied her triumphed over the sadness of her anticipated destiny.

They were already seated at table, when Fred Bryant came in, with the freedom of an old acquaintance. His cheek was flushed, and his manner betrayed the burden on his mind. Sometimes he would sit silent, and not seem to hear the words addressed to him; then, starting from his reverie, he would talk with a seemingly careless rattle that he had never before ventured on, at least in that company.

Tea was over at last, and the good Livingstons, pitying the young man, saw no reason why they should deny him the private interview with Lizzie which he evidently desired. So the husband took up his evening paper, and the wife withdrew on the plea of family cares. A window opening to the floor communicated with a piazza, and Fred, passing through, asked Lizzie some question about the beautiful honeysuckle that overhung it. As she followed, and before she could answer, he exclaimed, in a vehement whisper,—

"Shame on the man who would tear that lovely vine away from where it has grown for years, and take it to wither and die around a slave-pen at the South!"

"O Fred," she answered, sadly, "I know what you mean; but he is my father. The vine belongs to him; and, perhaps," she added with a reverent look, "God means the vine to yield some shelter to the poor tenants of the slave-pen."

"You shelter them!" he replied. "Dear enthusiast, you will need shelter yourself; and I can give it to you.

Will you not take it? I cannot bear it, either for myself or you, that you should go South with this — this man, if he is your father."

"Alas, Frederick, if it was right for me to wish to stay, I have no choice. He has every right, by the laws of God and man; and my refusal would only make unhappiness and discord, without accomplishing its object. I should only go as a prisoner, instead of a daughter."

"Nay, I would keep you as a prisoner," said he, with a fond smile; "a prisoner such as I am myself, fettered by love."

"Love's chain reaches far," said she. "If we are parted in person, we may be together in spirit."

"Ah," he replied, "that gives me some comfort. But what will come to you when so far off? Your father dislikes me, and I cannot pretend to like him; and to you new scenes will bring new attractions."

"Frederick!"

"O, forgive me. I cannot distrust you. But I can and must fear for you. You do not know the nature of the scenes to which you are going. Do you know the business your father carries on?"

"Yes, Fred, I found out to-day that he not only owns slaves, but deals in them. O Fred, you have given your noble, free, manly heart to the daughter of a slave-trader."

"No, no," he answered; "not his daughter. He gave you up in childhood; he disgraces you and tyrannizes over you now. No, you are Lizzie Livingston, not Betsy Witham. And, before to-morrow evening, I will call you, if you will let me, by another name." He stooped and whispered, " Lizzie Bryant."

She started and trembled. " O Fred, do not speak of that. You know it cannot be."

" It can be, very well, dearest. Such things are done every day. We are but twenty miles from the borders of another state, whose laws are less strict than ours are ; or at least they are construed so as to allow the marriage of persons from this side the line, without license or certificate. Do but say the word, and we will be on our way there in the morning, with one of the same fast horses that your father is so fond of driving."

" O Frederick, it cannot be. Besides my father's claims, I should be setting aside those of my kind friends here — my true father and mother they often seem to me."

" They are such indeed, dear Lizzie. And do not doubt that what I propose will have their approval. I must not tell them, for they are bound in honor to oppose it ; but when it is done, they will rejoice to keep you near them, and thank me for cutting the Gordian knot that they could not untie."

" No, Fred, it must not be. They would be suspected of having betrayed their trust ; they would be involved in a deadly quarrel with my father, and so would you be. And they would feel that I had not rightly returned their love and confidence. No, dear Fred, my duty is plain; and I feel that God has given me strength to do it. I have said in his presence, Come what will, I will be a faithful daughter."

"O, Lizzie, am I nothing to you, then?"

"You are every thing to me, Fred, that duty will let you be. I see I must take Richard Lovelace's words on a girl's lips, and say, —

'I could not love thee, dear, so much,
Loved I not honor more.'"

He paused a moment, and said, "You are right, and I am wrong. It should be the knight that says that, not the lady. I am ashamed that you should have to say it to me. How strange it is I must love you more for your refusing me! Well, I must wait, and it is some comfort that the road south is as open to me as it is to your father."

"But, Fred, you would not sacrifice your prospects, your business, your duties here, to follow me to that region. You cannot approach me there openly, with my father's approval, and you surely would not do it secretly."

"Dear, I will do nothing that you or Lovelace would be ashamed of. I will try to prove that I am worthy of you, and that I have caught something of your spirit. Do not fear from me any further proposal of a runaway marriage."

"Then you forgive me, Fred?" she asked, as Mrs. Livingston's voice reminded them of the increasing coolness. His answer is not recorded; but hand in hand they reëntered the parlor, and peace was in their hearts as they joined with their honored friends in the evening prayer.

CHAPTER VIII.

TRAVELLING SOUTH.

IT was not without extreme pain that Mr. and Mrs. Livingston yielded to the necessity of relinquishing their adopted daughter. Accustomed for years to consider her as their own, they felt that with her they should lose the very light of their house. For her, too, they felt a deep solicitude, which was not entirely relieved by the patient acquiescence she yielded to what she recognized as duty. Yet this went far towards strengthening them to bear the trial; and Lizzie nerved herself the more, in order to spare pain to her benefactors. Once, indeed, she was found in tears, and, when questioned, made no secret of her feelings. Mrs. Livingston's tears flowed with hers, till Lizzie left grieving for herself, and sought to console her protectress. "We can bear it, dear, if we think that you are happy," said Mrs. Livingston; "but if you feel so about it, we cannot consent; something must be done to prevent it."

Lizzie heard, and took her resolution. Her father's natural claim, her mother's wish, were enough of themselves to show her what was right. Henceforth she curbed every expression of sadness. No more tears were shed till the moment of parting swept away all restraint, and excused the feeling it indulged.

Mr. Livingston had attempted more than once to converse with Witham; but his repugnance to the man was such that only a few sentences could be interchanged in peace. Had each felt the other to be his equal, they would have had a violent quarrel; but the gentleman held his temper in restraint, lest he should disgrace himself by a contest with a man like Witham; and the slave-dealer could not quite overcome the consciousness of inferiority.

Mrs. Livingston was more successful in her attempts to converse. On the subject of claiming his daughter, Witham was indeed inflexible; and, as Lizzie was prepared to yield, there was, in regard to that, no more to be said.

But Mrs. Livingston endeavored to explain to the father in what respects his daughter would need forbearance and tenderness. She spoke of Lizzie's repugnance to the slave system, avoiding arguments which might exasperate, but pleading the difference between southern and northern habits of thought; and urged strongly that Witham should carry out his expressed intention to enter another mode of life, and have no more to do with the business he had thus far pursued. She tried to interest Mrs. Witham to the same purpose, and to secure a feeling of friendliness towards Lizzie in the heart of one on whom her comfort would so greatly depend. She was encouraged by finding that the step-mother was a woman of kinder feelings, and even of better principles, than she had feared.

The time of parting had come. Mrs. Livingston had placed in Lizzie's hands the few relics of her own mother that had been preserved, and had expressed, by many a parting gift, her own deep affection for the child she was about to lose. Among these, her own Bible, the one she used in her daily reading, seemed the thing nearest to herself to give to the daughter of her heart; and, by a mark between the leaves, and in the margin, she pointed out the text, "When my father and my mother forsake me, then the Lord will take me up." The farewell scene was over, and Witham, proud of his daughter, and softened by the success of his wishes, determined to do what he could to make her southern home agreeable to her.

It was towards sunset, about a week after, that the stage coach which contained the party entered the streets of Richmond. Their fellow-passengers, a Mrs. Compton and her two daughters, returning from Philadelphia to their home in Georgia, directed the driver to take them to the Powhatan House; but Witham knew that his own standing was not such as to obtain him and his party admission there. He named, therefore, another hotel, and they parted, Mrs. Compton with a distant bow to Mrs. Witham, and the girls with a smile to Lizzie.

"There, I am glad to have them out," said Witham. "Regular quality, that think themselves up to my lord and my lady, as I used to see in old England. They may have the grand house to themselves if they will; we shall do as well, I guess, with Jim Carpenter at the "Old Dominion."

And so they swept round the base of the hill, where stands, in its grand position, the Capitol, — its noble proportions borrowed by the taste of Jefferson from the Roman temple at Nismes, but its classic grace somewhat marred by the modern necessity of windows.

The next morning, as Lizzie, under her father's escort, was visiting the objects of interest in the city, they entered this building, and found themselves before the statue of Washington, by Houdon, which adorns its centre. Another party were standing near it, and they recognized their fellow-travellers of the day before. The younger Miss Compton looked at Lizzie with a friendly glance, but the other ladies did not appear to recognize her.

"It is considered," said a gentleman who accompanied the Comptons, "to be the best likeness there is of Washington."

"I believe there is one that rivals it," said Mrs. Compton, "one found on a piece of pottery, which proved admirably correct."

"So," said the gentleman, "it was promoted from its humble place on the side of a pitcher, and framed in gold."

"Like a village maiden made a queen," said the elder Miss Compton.

"Would you like to attend the drawing-room of such a queen, Miss Compton?" said the gentleman.

"Hardly in real life, Mr. Bruce. I should be afraid the vulgarity would show itself on the throne."

"Our English friends are right in that," said Mr. Bruce. "High birth is the security for high culture and high honor."

"And yet we find interesting characters sometimes," said Miss Compton, thoughtfully, "in strange connection. That sweet girl, you know, Emma, that was with us yesterday."

"What," said her mother, "travelling with those ———"

"Mamma, mamma," interposed Emma, hastily, "here is the young lady we were speaking of."

"Bless me!" said Mrs. Compton, "what was I —— How do you do, my dear? My daughter was just speaking of you. Isabella, I believe we shall not have time to stay longer." And the party retreated, the girls looking kindly, but rather shyly at their late fellow-traveller.

"Why, Betsy," said Witham, "I believe we've driven her ladyship away! So much for the land of liberty and equality!"

"With all that *he* did for it," said Lizzie, looking at the statue. "Pride and exclusiveness among the whites, and oppression over the blacks!"

"As to the blacks," said Witham, "they are meant to

be oppressed, as you call it; they ain't fit for nothing else. But I should think these folks thought we was niggers too, by the way they run away from us."

"What they think of us matters little," said Lizzie, "if we do our duty wherever we are placed."

"Well, I hope to be placed out of their way, at any rate," said Witham. "But come, let's go to that church you wanted to see."

It was the Monumental Church; and, after an approving glance at the general appearance of the building, they stopped beside the monument in the porch, and Lizzie read to her father the inscription, commemorating the dreadful catastrophe which occasioned its erection — when the theatre that stood on that spot took fire, and nearly a hundred persons, including the governor of the state, perished in the flames. As they heard anecdotes told of the mutual devotedness of some among the sufferers, "It was not so hard," thought Lizzie, "to perish, if the loved one was at their side."

The next moment she heard the sentiment, in almost the same words, from a voice near her, and looking round, saw that it was Isabella Compton who spoke. The sadness of her look and of her tone showed that she too was one who had suffered. They understood each other's sympathy in a moment.

"You feel as I do," said Miss Compton, in a low voice.

"I had just formed the same thought," said Lizzie.

"Yet I was afraid it was selfish. Ought we to take comfort in our own sufferings because a friend suffers too?"

"I was thinking I should have liked to share his fate," said the young lady, "not to have drawn him into mine. The friend I had in mind was lost at sea."

"O, I can feel for you," said Lizzie. "Your case is harder than mine."

"You have had sorrow, then? I thought so."

"I am going away from where I have been brought up, and I leave those behind whom I love very much."

"How could your parents let you go with such ——"

"Don't finish your sentence. He is my father!"

She spoke neither angrily nor ashamed, but in deep distress. She began to realize how her father was regarded; and she could not, as at the first moment, charge it upon pride and exclusiveness.

Miss Compton looked surprised. "Your father?" said she; "I am sorry — I did not mean to say any thing rude."

Her mother, who had been talking with Mr. Bruce, now noticed them, and called Isabella in a tone of some sharpness. The young lady, as she turned away, said, "I hope we shall meet again."

"Your mother does not," thought Lizzie. "Well, I have not been used to be so shunned; but, if all turn against my father, the more need for me to stand by him." And she felt a sudden gush of that filial love which she had prayed for, and had blamed herself that she could not more deeply feel.

CHAPTER IX.

LIFE IN XENOPHON.

XENOPHON, the chief town of Saunders County, Alabama, was reached at length, and Lizzie entered her southern home. She found it in outward appearance better than she had anticipated. The house was of that pattern which was then all but universal for houses of the middle class, two parlors with folding doors, and an entry at the side. It was of two stories, and the brick chimneys stood out from the wooden walls, as if the builder had forgotten them at first, and added them after the rest of the house was finished. There was a grass plat before the door, somewhat weedy; but this might be from the recent absence of the owner. About thirty feet in the rear stood the building for the work and lodging of the house servants; and on one side was an enclosure, surrounded by a high wall, and containing the jail, a building of brick, divided into two rooms for the male and female subjects of Witham's traffic. Lizzie shuddered as she looked at it; but she was upheld by her father's promise to relinquish the business, and by the determination to do what was in her power, in the mean time, to diminish the miseries that slavery brought.

Three of the servants, a mother and her two children, had been left by Witham at the neighboring tavern during his journey to the North, paying for their humble board and lodging by such services as they could render. These were of small account during most of the season, as there were enough without them; but at the time for picking cotton, the tavern-keeper was glad to have the command of three capable "hands." The woman, Rachel, surprised Lizzie at first by the strange jargon which she spoke, and by her extreme ignorance of every thing beyond her lowly employment; but her young mistress soon found her to be affectionate and faithful. The children, Nancy and Peter, about fifteen and thirteen years old, seemed as intelligent as white girls and boys of similar age, and full of merriment, which sometimes was obstreperous.

Wishing both to make herself of use, and to cultivate a pleasant feeling towards herself on the part of the slaves, Lizzie began by doing, as she had done at Mr. Livingston's, a part of the household work. But she soon found that this was entirely contrary to Rachel's notions of propriety.

"No, no, young missis," said the woman, as she found her sweeping her own room; "what for you hab nigger, me and Nancy, for you to go work yoursef? No, no;

gib ole Rachel de broom; you go down dar, play de pianny." She spoke so earnestly, that Lizzie saw that it was not merely the pretence of humility, but that the woman was actually uneasy at seeing a member of the white family working, as at something which was not proper.

The pity which she felt for their servile condition was diminished for a time by finding how happy they appeared to be. She recalled the remark she had heard from Dr. Solesby, that gayety in degradation is painful to witness, because it shows that the degradation has entered into the soul. Yet she could not but be thankful for even this outward alleviation of the lot of the bondman.

She observed in them all, and in the young girl Nancy especially, that love of bright colors which is characteristic of the race. One Sunday afternoon, Nancy came up stairs to her, decked in a profusion of hues, and on Lizzie's good-natured notice how brightly she was dressed, replied, " Tank you, missis; I only comed up to be complimized."

For two or three weeks Nancy was absent, her services being wanted at the hotel. The day after her return to the house, Lizzie heard from the lower regions the loud lament of a child under correction; and, on her coming down to inquire, the mother told her, that she " had to crack Peter a little." The poor fellow's trouble came from his ambition. During Nancy's absence, he had been allowed to take her place in setting the table; and when she returned, and undertook to resume her duties, he resisted the change with so much passion as to occasion Rachel's resort to the rod.

Lizzie's desire to do good led her quickly to entertain the thought of teaching these children to read. She was not at the time aware of the laws against such instruction. She spoke of it first to Nancy, who eagerly embraced the offer. Peter was indifferent at first, but, when he found out that Nancy was going to learn, his ambition to be equal to his sister was excited; and, that no motive might be wanted, his mother asked Lizzie to tell her if he did not learn well, and she would " crack him."

The matter was almost settled, when it occurred to Lizzie, that she ought not to undertake such an office in the family without consulting her step-mother. The intercourse between them had not been intimate, the restraint natural to the relation in which they stood being increased by the difference in education and habits of thought. But Lizzie was desirous to do all that might be expected of her, and felt conscious of having done wrong in going as far as she had, without the knowledge of the mistress of the family. Good-natured Mrs. Witham received her apology and request with some surprise, but gave her consent with indifference, though she told Lizzie it was " agin the law." " But laws," said she, " isn't nothing in one's own house. I've know'd lots of people have taught their niggers to read — folks that hadn't nothing else to do, I reckon, or they wouldn't have wasted their time so. So you do jes' as you please, Miss Betsy; perhaps you'll kind of like it, for it must be mighty lonesome for you here."

Armed with this permission, Lizzie began her task. The children were bright and obedient, and soon began to feel an interest in her instructions. Their young mistress was happy in the feeling of usefulness, and circumstances around her seemed more favorable than she had dared to anticipate. Her father and his wife, though unpolished, were kind; his habits of conduct and language had been kept under restraint by her presence; a few of the young people of the village had offered their acquaintance to Lizzie, and she did not yet know that they were not the first either in character or education. She saw differences, indeed, in all around her, from her own dear New England home; but her expectations had been so moderate, that the difference was less than she had supposed. As the season advanced, too, she noticed with delight the proofs of a genial climate in the lengthened beauty of the autumn and the absence of northern snow and sleet. Letters came frequently from the kind friends she had left, and, though they saddened her by some of their allusions, she was able to reply to them in a manner that showed that her submissive mind had found many sources of cheerfulness. But her peaceful sky was soon overcast.

One morning she was awakened early by a burst of

clamorous grief, which filled the house. As she rose in bed, and tried to imagine what the cause could be, Rachel came into the room sobbing and wringing her hands.

"O Miss Betsy, Miss Betsy, Nancy's gone! Nancy's done gone away!"

"Nancy gone away! Why, Rachel, what do you mean? Wasn't she at home last night?"

"O, yes, missis, but she's done gone; she's in de yard."

"In the yard, Aunt Rachel! Why, if she's in the yard, she can't be gone."

"In de *jail* yard, missis. De massa hab took her off to sell. O Miss Betsy, could you speak to de massa for de poor nigger gal, for de poor ole aunty, dat hab no oder chile but little Peter, and de four dat's away in Lou'siana?"

"Father's taken her off? My poor little Nancy! I'll go this instant, Rachel! But how do you know she has gone?"

"La, missis, de massa call Nancy up in de entry, and he put on de lock-ums on her arms, and tote her right off; and de chile scream, and he tell her hush, and slap her on de face."

"O, my father, my father!" said Lizzie, with tears not less bitter than those of the slave.

Dressing herself hastily, she went in search of Witham. The scene between them was too painful to be described. Lizzie's indignation burst the bounds she had determined to observe as those of filial duty; and finding entreaties vain to change her father's purpose of selling the girl, she gave free utterance to her feelings with regard to the system of slavery, the trade, and those engaged in it. But she soon found that in the war of words she was no match for the man whose anger she thus provoked. He answered her with a storm of abuse and profanity; and the unhappy girl fled to her own room, and wept there alone.

She remained there the greater part of the day. The feeling of terror with which she had heard her father's outburst of passion, gave way, ere long, to a sense of utter desolation. She had failed in her attempt to rescue Nancy; she recognized, for the first time fully, the odious character of her father's trade; she had heard the language he used when excited, in all its brutality and its blasphemy; and, worst of all, her conscience reproached her that her own ungoverned anger and unfilial words had led to this frightful exhibition on his part, and had made a breach between them, which might probably be fatal to her influence for good, either to him or others.

To her religious mind, however, this last thought brought the means of comfort. Guilty as her father was, she herself was not without blame. If it added to her sadness to feel that, far from earthly friends, she had broken the law of her heavenly Parent, the way, at least, was open to his throne of mercy. With tears, no longer of passion or of terror, but of penitence, she sought forgiveness; but, as she rose from her knees, she felt that her pardon from above would not be complete until she had received that of her earthly father. Wrong as his conduct was, he was her father still. There was the divine command to honor him, and she must do it by confessing her fault.

But would he not then be strengthened in his wrong course? Would not all her protest against his conduct go for nothing? It might be so, she thought; she would try to prevent it; but, if her influence with him was lost, the fact must be accepted as a part of her punishment.

She had reached this conclusion, and was thinking how best to make her combined confession and protest, when she heard a knock at her door, followed directly by her step-mother's call, —

"Betsy, Betsy dear, it's three o'clock, and you haven't been to breakfast nor dinner."

Lizzie opened the door, and the sight of the kind, anxious face stirred again the fountain of tears.

"There, don't cry, Betsy. Father was real angry; but he's gone away, and I thought I'd see what had come of you."

"O, mother, I am afraid I have done very wrong."

"Yes, you have, to stay up in your room so long, a taking on, and not eating a mouthful of victuals. It'll make you sick if you go on a doing so."

"O, I did not mean that. I meant that I spoke to father in a wrong way."

"Well, now, Betsy, I'm real glad to hear you say so. A father's a father, after all, and to be so dreadful angry with him, just because he goes and sells his own nigger——"

"But I can't think that right," said poor Lizzie, anxious to be true to both her duties. "Please, ma'am, tell me, what has become of the poor child?"

"Well, now, I'll tell you," said her step-mother, with a look and voice that seemed to promise well. "You see, father was a going to sell her to that man that was here yesterday. He's a travelling trader, going to Mississippi. But I didn't like to send her off so fur, and I talked to him some about it, and he was a thinking of selling of her somewhere round here, when you spoke to him. You went at him so strong, he got mad, and swore he would sell her to the Mississippi man, any how. And so he went and done it."

"And it is my fault then, my passion, my unkindness, that sent the poor child away! O, poor Nancy, poor Rachel!"

"Why, bless your heart, Betsy, don't begin taking on again. John,—I mean father,—he sold the gal; but I let Rachel go out, and she asked all around, and she begged, and she prayed; and at last she got Squire Adams to buy Nancy of the Mississippi man. And, I reckon, father isn't sorry, after all."

"Squire Adams?"

"Yes; the gentleman that has the cotton warehouse

out on Main Street. He said he'd have Nancy to wait on his wife. And so she'll stay in town, and see her mammy every now and then."

"O, I am so glad!" said Lizzie. "But," she added after a pause, "I wish it had been father that bought her back again."

"Well, I don't see what difference that makes; for the gal's here, and all's ended well. And now, you wash your face, and come and get ready to speak to father when he comes back."

With her homely mediation, and Lizzie's humble confession of the wrong of her passionate words, Witham was won to say, "Well, well, never mind. But, look here, Betsy, once for all, I won't have none of your interfering atween me and my niggers."

His daughter was too crestfallen to reply; and so, as has happened in many another instance, the less offender was condescendingly forgiven by the greater.

CHAPTER X.

A STAGE COACH AND ITS PASSENGERS.

THREE years had passed since the conversation recorded in our last chapter, when, along the most direct road from Charleston to New Orleans, a vehicle was seen advancing, of a description which is now seen no more. It was a mail coach, but not such as the well-caped Jehu drives from an English inn, nor such as those that from their birthplace on the Hudson spread far and wide the glories of modern Troy. Straight built, long, heavy, and without a door, its anterior portion was occupied, besides the black driver and a white boy, by piles of trunks and mail bags, while behind this barricade sat the passengers, suggesting, to the mind of any one who might catch a glimpse of them, the inquiry how they had ever got in, and how they could possibly ever get out. The one we now speak of was approaching the end, not indeed of its journey for that day, but of its term of service on that road; for the word had gone forth, a new contract had been formed with the post-office department, and the

Troy-built stage that was to take its place was already on its way, destined to be superseded in its turn by the rattling car and screaming locomotive.

Slowly and with labor the horses dragged the heavy vehicle, not over, but through the thick clay of the road. At length the clay was varied by a large stone, and after a terrible jolt, the passengers were aware that something in the foundation of their moving prison had given way.

"Dat axle done broke agin!" said the negro driver. "Here, Mas' Tom, take de reins; I must get sumfin' to mend him."

The needed aid was quickly obtained in the form of a rail from the neighboring fence, and this being placed in position, April—for that was the driver's vernal name—resumed his place of command.

"I wonder," said one of the passengers, "how one of their fine new stages would have stood such a jolt as that. It's all nonsense, putting those frippery things on these roads of ours. I've a good mind to keep the old line running as an opposition. Don't you think people have got sense enough to support it?"

The man whom he addressed smiled dubiously at the ardor of his conservative friend, and suggested that it would be hard to keep up an opposition, as the new line had got the contract for carrying the mail.

"Well," said the old contractor, "I s'pose they're bound to make a trial; but I should like to see how long it will be before they break those gimcrack things all to pieces, and come to me to buy my old solid stages."

Behind this disinterested lover of the past sat a couple of young men, who exchanged amused glances, and continued their own conversation. They could speak with the more freedom, as the others were absorbed in theirs.

"So, George," said one of them, "you really like this southern country better than you expected."

"So well, Fred, that, but for family ties, I would as willingly find my home here as any where. Some of the customs I have been used to, for you know I was partly brought up at the South. I find many kind friends, and there are many opportunities to do good, which, you know, in my profession if in any, ought to be thought of. The greatest objection is the social system prevalent here."

"You mean slavery," said Fred. "As to that, I confess, it does not strike me as offensively as I expected. I think as I always did, and trust I always shall, about the injustice of it; but there does not seem to be as much suffering as I had feared. On the contrary, the blacks seem remarkably light-hearted. One would not suppose, to see them, that there was such a thing as slavery."

"Perhaps you thought as one man did that I heard of — that all slaves wore literal iron chains; so, when he came to Charleston, and saw the negroes going about the streets, he thought they were all free blacks, and asked where the slaves were."

"No; I own that Charleston gave me an unfavorable impression of the system, not on account of the blacks, but of the whites. There seemed to be a sense of insecurity. The military police, a sentinel even posted in every church door on Sunday; the drum-beat at evening; the Citadel as a place of defence in case of insurrection, — all told a tale as of people living on the verge of a volcano. But the negroes themselves seemed happy enough, and some of them well enough off too. The hotel I stopped at, the most fashionable there, they told me was kept by a black man."

"And did they tell you that he had to get a pass signed by one of his boarders, in order to go abroad after nine o'clock at night? No; Jones is one of the exceptions that prove the rule. Here and there, a free negro may be petted, but he is still kept under."

"Why, George, I didn't expect to hear a southern minister, like you, talk like an abo—."

"Hush!" said George, checking his friend more by his gesture than by his voice. "Don't pronounce that dreaded word in southern hearing. But do not misunderstand me, either. I am not vain enough to think of revolutionizing society; and while I live with the southern people, and eat their bread, I should think it base treason to say a word that would really endanger their safety; but it is another thing to maintain that their system is all right."

"But how can you endure to live here, if you don't think it right?"

"Do you suppose that Paul liked the despotism of Nero? Yet he endured to live under it, and without saying a word directly against it; but he was constantly sowing the seed of that heavenly plant before whose growth despotism and sla— all forms of oppression must fade and die."

"You think the favorable view is superficial. What then lies under the surface?"

"More than I can tell with safety here; more than I could tell you any where. But to touch one of the most obvious points; last week I married a negro couple. The wedding was very prettily got up; the kitchen was perfectly neat, and the guests assembled in it — all slaves — were neatly dressed; the women perhaps a little too showily. Cake and wine were handed round, as if it had been in the parlor. And yet, when I said, 'Whom God hath joined together let not man put asunder,' I felt as if I had uttered words of impious mockery."

"But why? People who treated their slaves so well would not set aside the marriage which they themselves had permitted."

"Probably not; but suppose a failure in business, or the division of the estate by death. Then the law of man comes in, sets aside the solemn warning of the Saviour, sends John to one master, Jane to another, three hundred miles off, and perhaps their children to a third."

"That, indeed, I had not thought of before."

"No; and so it is with unnumbered bearings of the system. The people who live under it cannot help these evils; they can only mitigate them by personal care and kindness; but no one dare assail the system itself, for all are convinced that in its destruction society itself would be overthrown."

"What will be the end of it all, then?"

"I cannot tell. I can but preach the gospel, teach the people the great law of love to God and man, and leave that to do the work gradually; but sometimes I think some tremendous convulsion will sweep the whole away. So I live on and try to do my best. I say little about slavery, but much about justice and charity to all; but it does move my indignation when a man from the North comes here boiling over with abolitionism, spends a month or two, and goes back declaring that he understands the whole subject, that the slaves are very well treated, and that those who object to the system are only fanatics."

"What's that about the abolutionist fanatics?" said one of the men in front.

"I was saying that some people changed their minds about slavery very soon after they come here," said the young preacher.

"If they don't change their minds, they'd better

change their tune, about the quickest," said the man. "What are they after, meddling with other folks' business? If I was to meet an abolutionist, I'd beat him as I would a nigger."

"I would advise you, gentlemen," said the other passenger, in a serious though civil manner, "not to talk much on such subjects while you are travelling; especially if, as I suppose, you are from the North."

"O," said the clergyman, "I am a Southerner in part, and a minister in a southern parish. As for my friend, I don't know but he is more southern than I am. I thank you for your hint, but I think we shall be safe."

"Still, sir, you must think also of the safety of others. These things are not to be spoken of in all companies," motioning with his hand towards the negro who drove their conveyance.

"If you mean April, I reckon he's pretty safe," said the stage proprietor. "I'm not a man to be afraid of my own niggers, but I fancy they're rather afraid of me. So the parson can talk on, and I'd rather like to have him show his hand."

His more gentlemanly companion turned half round, and gave a quick glance of caution to the young minister, then changed the conversation by the abrupt question, "What's cotton now in Savannah?"

"Riz," said the other; "cotton's riz; and that's good news. There's some trouble about the crop abroad. One man told me he'd heard say that the Grand Packer of Egypt had hung up his pestle, and swore he wouldn't pack another bale."

The gentleman laughed. "A new meaning to the title," said he. "Bashaw, pacha, packer, — Bluebeard metamorphosed into a laborer to fill cotton bales! By the way, gentlemen, did you ever see a finer sight in the way of culture than a cotton plantation? Look over there, if you can see between April and the boy, at that prospect, spreading far and far away, with no fences to divide it — all the property of one man. All that verdure will in a few weeks be dotted with white, from the opening bolls; and that white is the talisman by which the South, if need be, can control the world."

"The absence of fences," said the young traveller, Fred, "reminds me of the meadows on the Connecticut, near Northampton. But those are not all one man's land; the wide field is divided into numberless little strips, with their various crops of grass, vegetables, and broom-corn. It is like the poet's imaginary golden age of England, —

'When every rood of ground maintained its man.'"

"O, as to that," said the Southerner, "unity of possession does not imply a scarcity of population. Come here when the bolls are fully open, and you will see the field swarming with men, women, and children, all gathering the treasure which gives bread to them as well as to their master."

The Northerner only replied by repeating thoughtfully, "Maintained its *man!*" The journey was pursued for a time in silence, and when conversation was resumed, it was on indifferent topics.

At the next town the travellers parted; the southern gentleman, for whom his own open carriage and well-dressed servant were waiting, turned off towards his plantation, which he courteously invited the young Northerners to visit when they should find it convenient; the stage contractor went to his house hard by; Fred pursued his journey to New Orleans; and his friend George went to visit the college at Tusculum, and spend the rest of his summer vacation among the hills in the northern part of the state.

CHAPTER XI.

TUSCULUM.

ABOUT half a mile from the three large brick buildings which formed the classic centre of the city of Tusculum, stood a house, before which a sign-board, swinging on a lofty mast, announced its name as the Eagle Hotel. The day after our travellers parted, the few idlers on the broad piazza observed a single passenger emerge from the stage coach. It was George Stevens, the young minister. A colored servant coming forward to take his baggage, he inquired if Mr. Witham was at home, as he had a letter of introduction to him. The man answered that his master was in, but was lying down. Going into the house, however, he returned directly, saying that his master would be happy to see the gentleman.

Mr. Stevens followed his guide, and had not far to go. The front door opened into a hall about twenty-five feet square, on the opposite side of which another door, in a partition of unpainted wood, led into a room of less width but greater length. Part of this was occupied by tables of coarse construction; but at the farther end, stretched on a cot, lay the burly figure of a man half dressed. His appearance indicated habitual and recent indulgence in liquor. Without rising, he opened the letter addressed to him, welcomed his guest, and introduced him to his wife and daughter. The former was younger than her husband, and apparently in very feeble health. The daughter, too, was pale; but this might be from the effect of a southern climate. There was taste in the choice and arrangement of her cheap and simple dress. There was an expression on her features, not so much of dejection as of seriousness — an expression which forsook her the moment she was spoken to, when she answered with a bright smile, or turned quickly to whatever work had been assigned her. Still, when the remark or the work was over, that expression would return.

The visitor soon had assigned to him a room adjoining that in which they were. It was, like the others, partitioned with unpainted boards; but what female taste could do with scanty means, had been done to render it comfortable. Mr. Stevens soon left it, and inquiring his way around the village, proceeded to distribute his letters of introduction, which in other instances were received under circumstances more promising than those of Witham, for the character of the persons to whom they were directed. He learned incidentally, in conversation, that the tavern-keeper had been in the place about a year and a half. Little seemed to be known of his family, but there was a feeling of pity for them, of that lukewarm kind which people express in behalf of those whom they cannot help, and with whom they do not desire to have any thing to do.

His letters were all distributed except the last, and with this he was directed to a house a little distance from the town, and surrounded by shrubbery. Reaching it by a path that wound pleasantly among trees, partly of the natural growth and partly of recent planting, he inquired for Professor Wheeler, and was received by a gentleman of middle age, who warmly welcomed him on the perusal of his letter of introduction. It was nearly the hour of the evening meal, and the guest was not suffered to depart until he had shared it. Another hour passed on, and, delighted with the intercourse of an intelligent family from his own section of the country, Stevens could scarce resist the urgent wish of his entertainer that he would transfer his baggage from the hotel, and make the professor's house his home while he should remain in Tusculum. It was resisted, however; and the young man returned in the evening to the Eagle.

He spent the next day in visiting the college, under the guidance of Professor Wheeler; and, for the two or three that followed, engagements of business or of courtesy occupied his mind and time. At length, however, the changing aspect of things at the hotel gave indication of great events about to occur. Stages arrived, not only of the primitive form which has been described, but exhibiting all the superiority of northern manufacture; while private conveyances, from the carriage to the saddle-horse, threw clouds of dust upon the road, and gave constant employment to the servants of the Eagle Hotel. Commencement day was approaching, and it was the more regarded, as the rival candidates for the office of representative in Congress had agreed to meet in Tusculum at that time, and give to the scholarly gathering something of the fresh interest of modern life, by a debate upon the principles of their respective parties.

The hotel, which Stevens had found comparatively deserted, was now thronged to overflowing. Our young clergyman was at first requested by Witham to allow another gentleman to share his bed: when night came he found that the privilege had been granted to a third, without the formality of again asking his consent; and morning brought into the room two others, who, having slept in some unimagined place, claimed a partnership in Stevens's room for their toilet for the day. Going forth, not very well pleased with this proceeding, he found dining-room and hall thronged with sleeping humanity. Some on cots, and some on the floor, the votaries of Tusculan learning or of Tusculan politics left it scarcely possible for the traveller to emerge into the daylight.

He lingered on the piazza till many of the sleepers came forth, and it was filled with a throng of men of various classes in society, some with cigars and some without, amusing themselves with whatever might occur. At one moment the means of entertainment was furnished by the editor of a newspaper in a neighboring city, who had mystified a countryman by a proposition which we will let him express in his own words: —

"I maintain," he declared, "that if a man is brought up from childhood on corn-bread, cabbage, and ham, and nothing else, he will be nothing else than corn-bread, cabbage, and ham."

"No," replied the countryman; "he will be flesh and blood and bones."

"But that flesh and blood and bone will be nothing but corn-bread, cabbage, and ham," exclaimed the disputant. "The man has eaten nothing but that, and nothing but that is in him."

A roar of laughter followed this argument, while the puzzled countryman declared that he could not explain it, but really it seemed to him that the man would not be either corn-bread, or cabbage, or ham.

Our clerical friend soon had occasion to perceive that his companions were as fond of practical jokes as of facetious arguments. Wishing for the exercise of riding, he had applied to Witham for the hire of a horse; and now, in obedience to his call, the animal was led out in front of the thronged piazza. It was a shaggy white beast, not much larger than a pony; and as the intended equestrian looked from it to the amused assembly, and again to the horse, it was evident that some one had been tampering with the sable groom to secure a little sport at the stranger's expense. A closer look assured him that the saddle had been merely placed on the animal's back, and not secured by a girth. In a quiet manner, as if not suspecting any wrong intention, he had the "mistakes" set right, and, properly mounted, took his morning ride.

Unwilling to encounter, on his return, those whose rudeness had prompted such treatment of an unoffending stranger, Mr. Stevens rode around the house in search of the stables, and dismounted there. He was returning to the main building, when his attention was atracted by the sound of weeping; and turning to the direction from which it came, he saw, by the grated windows, that he was in the vicinity of a negro jail.

"O, what shall I do?" were the words he caught, interrupted by sobs. "What shall I do? Massa's gone and sold me, and poor Joe don't know nothing about it. O poor Joe! when he come next time, I no there! O poor Joe, poor Joe!"

Stevens quickened his step to pass the jail, but this only brought him nearer to it, and the voice he next heard kept him where he stood.

"Don't cry, Aunt Sally; I'll do all I can for you. Perhaps father can keep you, or sell you here, so you won't have to go away. O, I know how hard it is to go away from home and friends."

"Lord bless your soul, Miss Betsy; you too good for dis world! O, please don't let your pa sell de poor nigger woman dat live only jes next door, and knowed you same as you was her own folks; please don't let him sell her to go away off to Texas. O poor Joe, poor Joe!"

The young minister yielded to a strong impulse to speak a word of comfort; pausing at the window, he said emphatically, "Trust in God;" then turned away, and went toward the main building. "Ah," said he to himself, "I can tell her to trust; yet God suffers these things to be, and I know there is but little hope."

It was with saddened heart that he prepared himself to witness the public exercises of the day. They were to take place in one of the churches of the village, and to this Stevens bent his way. As he advanced, he saw the procession of the faculty, students, and invited guests issuing from the college grounds. A sign from Professor Wheeler invited him to join it, and he fell into the ranks with the gentlemen of his own profession, among whom he found some with whom he was slightly acquainted.

Stevens had wished to be present at this occasion, to compare the aspect of a southern college with that of the northern institution where he had himself been educated; but it was some time before he could notice any thing, except in its connection with what he had overheard in the morning. The prayer, which asked God's blessing on the exercises and those who engaged in them, seemed to him to rise burdened by the weight of the guilt and misery around; and the references which the young orators made, in glowing language, to the greatness of their country, "the home of freedom, the refuge of the oppressed," seemed to him blind self-deception or bitter mockery.

As he recovered his self-possession, he could not but give credit to the young men before him for a degree of natural grace and ease as speakers, which compared well with his own college companions. He noticed among their names some which were familiar to him from their connection with the past history of the state or of the nation; and he saw from the rank which these held, and from their appearance in the exercises, that the reputation of their families for talent was not likely to be impaired in them.

"At the North," said he to himself, "the first scholar would probably be some youth from an obscure country village — one who had his fortune to make. Here it is the descendant of an old historical family. Is it because the advantages of earlier education are more generally extended there, or because the whole spirit of southern institutions is more aristocratic?"

The last oration was delivered; the band pealed forth their music; the president addressed the graduating class, counselling them to consider the education they had received as only preliminary to the advance they were yet to make, and to consecrate all advancement to duty, their country, and their God. In simple form, without square cap or Latin phrase, the degrees were conferred; and in a concluding prayer the divine blessing was asked on those who now went forth from those quiet shades into the busy world. Mr. Stevens, accepting an invitation from one of the leading men of the state, found himself one of a large company, and apparently the only one who was not a native. A few remarks were made upon the literary exercises of the day; but this subject soon gave place to that of politics. Among the gentlemen present were two or three whose dress varied from the general uniformity of black. They were clad in brown homespun cloth, which they willingly exhibited to the inspection of those around; and much admiration was expressed for the fineness of its texture, and the patriotic spirit with which its wearers endeavored to encourage the industry of their own state. Stevens could not fail to perceive — what was indeed by no means new to him — the existence of a deeply-seated jealousy of northern enterprise, and dread of northern influence. His own treatment, however, was highly courteous. Some curiosity was apparent to learn the impression which the commencement exercises had made upon his mind, and those who spoke with him were gratified to find that it was decidedly favorable.

Among others present was the governor of the state. His conversation with the young stranger turned upon the action of the legislature in distributing by lottery a large territory recently obtained from its Indian owners. Stevens remarked that in the North such an extensive acquisition would have been kept as a source of public wealth, only small portions being disposed of at a time.

"We have wished to dispose of it," said the governor. "We want to have the state all occupied. So long as there are large portions of unsettled land, our people will be restless, and civilization will not advance; but when the territory is generally filled up, they will turn their attention more to the arts of quiet life."

The clergyman ventured, with some of this courteous company, to speak of the Eagle Hotel, and of his discovery of the morning. What he said was received with uneasiness, and replied to with earnest assurances that such things were not the genuine marks of a system, but its unavoidable evils. "You are aware," said one, "that the state prohibits the importation of negroes for sale."

"I know it," replied Stevens, "but where I live the negroes are brought to the opposite shore of the river; purchasers have but to cross the bridge and make their bargains, and all objection to the importation of the slave ceases."

"This girl," said their entertainer, "must be a slave of Mr. Johnson. He is ruined by his dissipated habits, and has no doubt been forced to sell her; and if I am not mistaken, her husband is on a plantation adjoining mine. I will see, Mr. Stevens, what can be done to prevent her being sent away. You northern people must not think that there is no humanity among us."

From the dinner table our traveller withdrew early.

He had received in the morning from a student a notification of his election as an honorary member of one of the college societies. For which of his merits this compliment had been conferred, he was yet in doubt; but as a meeting of the body in question was announced for three o'clock, he turned his steps in the direction indicated, and soon entered the hall of the society.

He found it filled, in part with students and in part with visitors, who, he had reason to believe, had received a similar honor to his own. There was much formality about the meeting, and a greater display of officers and regulations than among those who have the business of mature life to transact. When the preliminaries were completed, the president of the society made a speech, which enlightened Mr. Stevens as to the reason of his membership. But when Stevens told about this journey afterwards, he smiled when he came to this point, and said he was not at liberty to disclose the proceedings of a secret society. He would add no more, but that he liked the Logomachian Society very well, and wished them all success in their honorable rivalry with the Philopolyglossian Fraternity.

CHAPTER XII.

THE EVIL EVERY WHERE.

THE young clergyman found the hotel nearly deserted when he returned to it, after a walk around the village. A public meeting, at which the rival politicians were to present their views, had drawn to it alike the visitors from abroad and the idlers of the place. Not disposed to join them, he was passing through the dining hall on the way to his room, when he saw there the daughter of his host, engaged in sewing, and stopped to ask if she had been present at the commencement exercises.

"No, sir," she replied; "I have been too much engaged, and if I had had time, should have had little spirit for such a gathering. You know about poor Sally."

"The negro woman who is to be sold? It was you, then, that I heard speaking with her as I passed?"

"Yes, sir; and you cannot think how much good your few words did to the poor creature. She was frightened at first, and I was startled to hear a voice so unexpectedly; but it seemed to us the more to be a message from above. 'Trust in God!' O, it is hard to do so, among so many trials and disappointments."

"You speak feelingly, Miss Witham. You sympathize deeply with your poor neighbor."

"I do, indeed, sir. She has lived near us here; and sometimes when mother has been sick, and I have felt depressed, that poor black woman's kind word has given me new strength to do what I ought."

"I should think your father, then, would be easily persuaded to keep her, and not send her away, as she seems to fear so much."

"Father cannot afford it. He only bought her to sell again, and must do so to pay what he owes for her."

"But cannot he form some plan to keep her here? Cannot you persuade him?"

"O, I wish I could," said the girl with tears. "But father is — is — I beg your pardon, I must not speak about him."

"Why, he loves you, certainly. He has taken great pains in your education, I should judge."

A burst of tears was her only reply. Stevens was embarrassed, not less than affected. But believing he understood the cause of her grief, and that it was a cause which she ought to control, he spoke, when she was somewhat recovered, with kind seriousness.

"I judge from your style of language and thought, that you have been educated at some excellent school, and probably at the North. Now, if so, it must be hard for you, I know, to come from such company as you there enjoyed, to this hotel, and its daily round of dull cares, and even of low life. But, my dear young lady, these common cares of life are God's appointment to us."

"I feel them to be such."

"And I hope you will feel, too, that the friends God has given us are to be cherished and valued according to his appointment. Try not to think of your father's faults; whatever they are, they proceed from a cause which is, alas! sadly common throughout the land. How many daughters have fathers who indulge this appetite for drink! If any thing can wean him away from it, it will be your love. Do not look down on him who gave you life, and who has taken, it is plain, such admirable care of you. It may have been ill-judged for him to educate you above the station he could place you in; but as for your sake he has spared no expense, and even denied himself your loved society ——"

"O, sir," said the weeping girl, "how little you know ——" She controlled her emotion by a strong effort, and continued, after a brief pause,—

"It is due to myself, sir, that I should tell you something of my past history. My parents were English people; my mother died in extreme poverty, in a village in New England, where my father had left her. Neither she nor any one knew where he had gone. I was taken by an excellent family, and brought up as their own.

My father came back after a year or two, but was satisfied to leave me with such good friends; and I saw but little of him till I was sixteen, when he came and claimed me. I thought it my duty to go with him, and I try to love and honor him as I ought; but, but — O, I can't speak of it;" and her self-control gave way again.

Here a female voice was heard calling "Betsy." The girl started, and withdrew hastily to an inner room. The minister remained a few moments lost in thought. Then, heaving a deep sigh, he said aloud, "Well, it is idle to grieve over troubles that I cannot mend. What shall I do to change these sad thoughts? The political meeting? No, it is almost over, probably; and if not, what do I care about it? Another walk? No; I am tired. Can't I write a letter? The huge inkstand at the bar can be borrowed, I suppose." Before many minutes had passed, he was engaged in describing the Tusculan commencement. He had not made much progress, however, when he heard the voices and the tread of many persons returning from the political meeting; and when some of his numerous room-mates entered, he yielded to necessity, and postponed the completion of his letter to a more favorable time.

The next day Mr. Stevens received a visit from the gentleman at whose house he had dined. They conversed at first upon the literary and political gatherings which had taken place; but the visitor appeared grave, and the young minister found that the burden of the conversation rested principally on himself. At length, however, with a sudden effort, Colonel Selwyn relieved his mind of the weight which was upon it.

"My dear sir," said he, "I never like to limit the freedom of discussion in my own house; but you must be aware that on one subject we are very sensitive. I regret the existence of slavery. I wish the blacks were all across the Atlantic Ocean, or beneath it, I hardly care which. But here they are, and we must be their masters, or they will be ours."

"I am aware," said Stevens, "of the difficulties that embarrass the subject. I know it will not do to discuss it in public, where the blacks might hear."

"In public! Certainly not. The next thing would be a negro insurrection, with all its unimaginable horrors. The safety of our homes, the lives of our wives and children, depend on our peremptorily putting down all agitation on the subject."

"And yet, sir, I have been surprised, sometimes, at the freedom with which Southerners themselves would speak upon it, seated at table, and with their slaves standing behind their chairs."

"Well, we can do as we please, and I suppose we are careless sometimes. Probably every master thinks his own slaves can be trusted. You have no idea, sir, of the attachment of these people. I would far rather sleep with my door unbolted on my plantation, than in the best hotel in any northern city."

Stevens smiled slightly at the contrast of this great security with the fear just before expressed. "I should be sorry," said he, "to have said any thing to offend those by whom I was received so kindly."

"O, you may be assured there was no offence. Only I would caution you that the same language would not do in all companies. The present, too, is an unfortunate time. Here are our fiery Carolina neighbors ready to leave the Union, if they can but get a few other states to join them. They profess that it is all on account of the tariff; but depend upon it, sir, slavery is at the bottom of it all."

"But why so, sir? The abolitionists, from all that I hear of them, are a very small, and very unimportant party at the North. Nay, I believe their best men are opposed to their being a party at all, and think they can work better by moral suasion than by political control."

"As for any thing that they can do, we may well despise it. We are not afraid of northern emissaries among us, though, if we caught them, we should deal with them in a pretty summary manner. But I will tell you where our danger lies. Every year, thousands of our people go to the North, some for business and some for pleasure. Now, though you have few avowed abolitionists, the whole feeling of your people is against slavery. Our young men meet it in your colleges, our merchants in your cities, and our pleasure-seekers at Newport and

Saratoga. If they adopt that feeling, and bring it back, we have the evil of anti-slavery introduced among ourselves. Now, all we can do to prevent this is to break off intercourse; and that can only be done by dividing the Union. This is the way our Nullifiers reason. For myself, I am a Union man."

"I suppose," said Stevens, "the subject is beyond any human management; but at least we can do something at times to alleviate the suffering it brings."

"You are right, sir; and that is what I want to do in the case you spoke of. In fact, I have seen Witham already about it. He puts a high price on the girl — higher than I can well afford to pay — because he thinks he can command more by selling her to Texas. But I think I shall effect it. He is too old and too dissipated to travel himself with his merchandise, as he used to; and I fancy that pretty daughter of his has made him a little ashamed of the business. If I can buy Sally, the man she calls her husband lives on the next plantation to mine; and, so long as they like one another, I shall not interfere."

"Then you think they are not really married?"

"O, married, as far as they can be. Some Methodist exhorter joined their hands, I suppose. But that sort of marriage they are continually breaking up, to form new ones. Your northern people think a great deal of our separating families; but in fact the families would not stay together if we let them."

"Is not that itself, sir, a consequence of the system?

Seeing that their marriages may be broken up at any time by their masters' will, they learn to regard them as of little obligation."

"May be so — may be so; but as you and I can't help the system, suppose we go and help this poor woman, if we can. She'll do better on my plantation than in Witham's jail; and, as for her husband, she may have him till they get sick of each other."

CHAPTER XIII.

THE GOLD REGION.

Part of a Letter.

* * * * *

I WAS interrupted at the last sentence, and have let a fortnight pass before continuing. Meantime I have been wandering about among the mountains and gold mines of Upper Georgia; and you, I trust, have had all success on that mysterious errand which has carried you to the place with the learned name. Whatever the attraction was to Xenophon, may you, in finding it, have realized your best hopes. I, too, have had my visions of beauty. But no, the matter is too serious for jesting. Let me tell you something of my travels.

I continued my journey from Tusculum on horseback. Shall I tell you how I purchased a horse, and, with the assistance of a kind friend, escaped being taken in? No; for you will not believe the assertion. Shall I tell you of my undertaking to ford a wide river, and unexpectedly finding that my horse was swimming? There had been a freshet, which I had not counted on; so, as the river came in the way of the road, in I went. When my steed got off his legs, I was a little startled; but he seemed to know what he was about, and I left the matter to him; so he brought me over in safety.

This stream was the boundary of the region acquired a few years ago from the Indians, and which has since been rapidly settled on account of its mineral wealth. It was not long after my aquatic experience that I entered the mining town of Orville. I wish it was possible to describe to you its appearance. The street was as thickly set with houses at its sides as with mud in its travelled portion; but such houses! Booths would be the more proper name. They were built extempore, some with boards placed vertically, braced together by a few that crossed them, so that they looked like great square hogsheads, if a hogshead could be square. In others, the boards or slabs were horizontal. Paint was absent, and whitewash was infrequent; but amid the scene, two regular frame-houses, partly built, looked gigantic and palatial by the contrast, and gave hint of what Orville is to be. As to the state of society here, it may be inferred from such anecdotes as this: A Methodist preacher came along, in the excellent spirit of that sect, — Heaven bless them for it, though I don't like all their ways, — and preached one Sunday in whatever hovel answers the purpose of their grand assembly room. At the conclusion of his services, when he had appointed another meeting for the evening, one of the audience rose, and gave notice that there would be a game at shuffle-board, at the same time, in the street in front — an announcement which was received with a storm of laughter and applause.

In this vicinity I spent several days, visiting the dwellings of some with whom I had been acquainted, or became so; and, so used was I at length to the rough log-cabins, which these settlers for the most part inhabit, that when I saw at last a log-house, with the interior whitewashed, — cleats of wood having been previously nailed over the interstices to keep out the wind, — it appeared to me absolutely stylish, by its contrast to the rest.

An object of much interest to me was to visit the gold mines. I went to several, and saw the process of obtaining gold, from the simplest form to those more complicated. The first who settled in the gold region used nothing more than a pan, in which they washed the gravel by the banks of streams, throwing out the contents of the pan by degrees, till at last some grains of the metal would be discovered mingled with sand in the bottom of the pan. These would be then taken into combination by quicksilver, forming a little button of the amalgamated metals. The process now generally in use is an advance on this, being that of rocking the gravel in a sort of slanting cradle, through which a stream of water is constantly made to pass. The water washes off the earthy particles, while the gold, sinking by its greater weight, is detained by bars nailed across the bottom of the cradle.

I visited, however, some places where the work was undertaken on a larger scale. In one, the gold is sought partly by rocking, as I have just described, the gravel being obtained from the borders of a stream. Elsewhere, on the same estate, literal mining had been carried on extensively, but thus far with no profitable result. Here was a hill, that had been perforated from side to side, and the work upon it abandoned; there lay the wreck of a steam machine that had proved unserviceable. At the time of our visit, the object of labor was to sink a shaft deep enough to strike upon a vein of gold, which, from the dip of the strata, was thought to lie beneath. But the work had been stopped half way by the bursting in of water; and this was to be drained off by means of ropes and buckets, before the labor on the mine could be resumed. We left, foretelling that the owner would use up on his profitless hill mine more than the results of his very profitable surface mine.

Not much more promising for immediate success was another which we visited, where a large gang of laborers were penetrating a rock, within which, it was supposed, lay a vein of gold. Tons of the broken rocks lay around, and from these, if there were steam power at hand to crush them, we were told that immense sums might have been obtained. At this place we asked the overseer if we could purchase any specimens of the ore. He replied that he had none himself to dispose of, — for if any of value were found, the negroes concealed them. "But," said he, "if you ask that fellow when I am out of the way, I dare say he will be able to let you have some." We laughed at his putting us in the way of eluding his own vigilance, and obtained some little specimens, in the manner indicated, without much difficulty.

This region may be considered as the gradual descent, towards the south of the great Alleghany chain. I cannot say that I think its scenery much improved by the log-cabins of the settlers, and the muddy work which defiles every stream whose gravel is thought to contain gold. But, if one can get a little way off from the settlers, he will find sights among these hills that possess a beauty and a grandeur all their own. Such was the scene I witnessed from the summit of the Currahee Mountain, a conical hill to the south of the gold region, up which I rode with a party of friends. Far and wide, east, south, and west, stretched below us, apparently to the very horizon, an unbroken forest. The clearings were so slight, in comparison with the vast space uncleared, that they passed unnoticed; and the minor elevations were lost, from the superior height of that on which we were. It seemed a perfect level, a green ocean, blending with the sky. Another spot to be remembered was the wondrous ravine of Tallulah Falls, where, stretched on the rock called the Devil's Pulpit, and looking over, we saw an eagle cleaving the air half way beneath us, while the forest lay far below his flight; then, raising our eyes, we mused whether mortal foot had ever trod that cavern among the rocks far off upon the other side. But O, Toccoa, pure, beautiful cascade, thou art my favorite! I was told this fall was hardly worth seeing after Tallulah, on account of its small volume of water; and should not have visited it, but that it lay nearly in my way. So I rode on alone, with my thoughts on far distant scenes, when, suddenly, raising my eyes, I saw, above the tops of the trees, a cliff with a veil of woven rain-drops thrown across its rugged face. I threaded the forest path, and soon stood beside the lakelet into which that veil descends; and there I dismounted, and lingered, I know not how long, looking at the gigantic rock, the lovely stream, and the shrubs that grew so daringly, as it seemed, in the very path of the descending waters. There is a wild Indian legend connected with this place, that a woman betrayed a portion of a hostile tribe to death, by leading them, in single file, through the woods to the precipice above, on which they came so suddenly that they fell over in succession, their screams of terror being lost, to those who followed, in the roar of the cataract.

But I must close. How much I have yet to tell you! I had not half finished even about the college, when those politicians came in upon me, with their State Rights and Nullification. But you shall hear all about it, when you come to my bachelor-home on your return; and I know not but I shall tempt you to follow my steps, when

I have told you the touching story of my landlord Witham's daughter. Poor girl, poor girl! Well, for details you must wait till we meet. Till then, farewell, with every good wish, from

     Your friend and chum,
       GEORGE V. STEVENS.

To FREDERICK W. BRYANT, Esq.,
  New Orleans, La.

CHAPTER XIV.

HASTY AND INCAUTIOUS.

IT so happened that Mr. Bryant, when he received his friend's letter in New Orleans, looked first at the last page, on which, in those days when separate envelopes were not, the direction was written. There he saw, written across the page, some words on the subject upon which, most of all, he desired information. A part had been covered by the seal; but enough was legible to show that his friend knew where Witham lived, and to excite the most painful feelings for the unknown trials which his daughter had had to encounter. "Why has not she written!" said Bryant to himself, as he hastily closed the letter, and made his escape from the hotel reading-room, where he had opened it, lest his agitation should be perceived. "Fool that I was, why did I not let Stevens know of whom I was in search? But thank God, I am on the track at last." A hasty perusal of the letter showed that this sentence was all that it contained upon the subject; and before evening the young man was on the way to Royalton, where his friend resided.

When, several days afterwards, the commodious stage-coach, which had now taken the place of the lamented "old line," rolled into the broad Main Street of that pretty town, and stopped before a handsome hotel, Bryant eagerly inquired for a conveyance to the lodgings of his friend, and was soon on his way to the summer suburb, where those citizens of Royalton, who did not visit the North during the summer months, took refuge when they could from the dust and the mosquitoes of the city. Past the double rows of Pride-of-China trees; past the upper market-house, which looked down the street to front its southern counterpart; past the dry channel called the Beaver Dam, filled with cypress trees, whose roots bulged forth into those strange excrescences called cypress knees, well known to southern ship-builders; past the long ascent of the hill, — he came at length to a wood laid out in streets, as few as possible of the trees being removed, to make way for the neat houses that sheltered themselves beneath the branches of those that remained. A turn of the road brought him in sight of the fair front of the United States Arsenal, which he had visited with his friend, examining curiously the block-house in the centre of its quadrangle, its substantial timbers pierced for musketry, in preparation to meet the threats of Nullification. At length the barouche drew up before a house among the trees, and, bidding his colored driver remain for a time, Bryant rang at the door, and was shown into the study of his friend.

"Why, Fred, how came you here? And how strange you look! What has happened?" said the clergyman, his first feeling of pleasure giving way to alarm.

Fred had seemed to his fellow-passengers from New Orleans the coldest of human beings. He had scarce spoken to them, or noticed when they spoke to him; and the negro who drove him from the hotel had mentally contrasted the Yankee's reserve with the condescending manners of some of his southern young masters. One thought had engrossed the traveller's mind, one intense anxiety; and now, when that was either to be relieved, or rendered still more painful, he turned deadly pale, and seemed scarcely able to support himself. Taking a chair, and trying to speak with composure, he said,—

"You wrote about a man named Witham, and the sad story of his daughter. Is she living? What do you know about them?"

"Witham," said the minister; "what, the tavern-keeper at Tusculum! The drunken brute! What can you know, or care, about him?"

"That was the place then? But about Lizzie: what did you hear of her, that made you write that her story was so touching?"

"My dear Fred, don't look so utterly distracted ——"

"Do, Stevens, answer my questions."

"Why, don't get out of temper, man."

"O, George, you can't think what this is to me."

"I can think it well enough, you bear of a lover.

Nothing but Cupid could make Fred Bryant lose his good manners. But I'll put you out of your pain, to some extent, at least. The daughter, whose name is not Lizzie, but Betsy, as I can tell from hearing her called by the voice of a she-dragon — I wish you joy, Fred, of your father and mother-in-law!"

"Never mind, George, only tell me about her. She is living with them yet then, and the fellow is keeping tavern in that Tusculum?"

"Tavern, with a little sprinkling of jail, besides. He deals in his fellow-creatures, in a small way. For pity's sake, Bryant, if you have done any thing so crazy as to fall in love with such a man's daughter, get over it as soon as you can. Remember your family, — your education, — what society expects of you ——"

"You do not know, George, that she is the adopted daughter of one of the best and most respectable families in my native town; and the only reason she is with this brute of a father, is her heroic sense of duty. But as to marrying her, that is not the question. If she is in suffering, or in danger, I must protect her. Tell me, — I say again, forgive my excitement, — but tell me all you know about her, and those that she is with."

Thus appealed to, Mr. Stevens gave an account to his friend of what he had seen and heard while at Tusculum, in which Witham's daughter was concerned; and, when Bryant left him, refusing his hospitable invitations on the ground of want of time, he went, provided with letters of cordial recommendation to Professor Wheeler of the college, and to Colonel Selwyn, the gentleman who had bought the slave Sarah, to prevent her from being sold away from her husband. Bryant had already, with great satisfaction, learned that Tusculum was the residence of Judge Hendrick, a gentleman who, when visiting the North, had been the guest of his uncle, and had taken an interest in Frederick himself as a schoolboy.

"Ah, my friend," said he, as he returned to the gate, and found the negro driver dozing on the front seat of the carriage, "I've kept you so long that you had to go to sleep? Well, never mind, since the horses have not run away with you. I should have been sorry to have had your neck broken in my service."

"Horse no run when I'm on de box, massa," said the man, "I wake up right easy." In his mind, he added, "Someting wake massa up too, I reckon. He done said more now dan de whole ride before. Dese Yankees strange folks."

"Do the people all move away from here after summer is over?" said Bryant.

"Most ob 'em do, but dere's some stay out at de Sand Hills all de year roun'."

"I should think it the pleasantest way, John. That's your name, isn't it? I think I heard them call you John."

"No, no, massa; my name's Toussaint."

"Toussaint! Strange they should give such a name as that! Do you know who Toussaint was?"

"No, massa, I didn't know it was a man at all. De massas names us niggers after most any ting comes to hand."

"Well, they named you after the greatest man of your race, and one of its best men too, I fancy; but he had a sad fate;" and, talking rather to himself than to the negro, he repeated the first lines of Wordsworth's sonnet;

"'Toussaint, thou most unhappy man of men!'"

"Wha' for dey use him so, massa?" asked the driver.

"He led the slaves of St. Domingo in an insurrection against the whites; and the whites afterwards took him prisoner, and carried him to a cold country, where they kept him shut up in a very cold, damp prison, till he died."

"Did Samingo do dat to him?"

"Who?"

"Massa say, Toussaint led de slaves ob Samingo."

"O, Saint Domingo. That was the name of the island — the country I mean — where Toussaint lived. The person that shut up Toussaint was Bonaparte — Napoleon Bonaparte. You have heard of him, haven't you?"

"Tink so," said the slave, dubiously; and added, with a furtive look at his passenger, "I reckon massa'd have stood by Toussaint when he done make dat resurrection. Massa wouldn't have seen 'em use him so."

"No, I hate to see a brave man oppressed."

"Maybe massa'd stand by de brack men now, if dey'd make a resurrection, jes' like in Samingo."

"What!" said Bryant, suddenly aware of the dangerous nature of his conversation. "No; it would be madness and wickedness both. The whites are so much stronger, it would be impossible to succeed; and it would be only filling the land with murder and rapine to no purpose. My good fellow, I ought not to have told you about Toussaint at all; but don't speak to any one of what I said to you; don't think of it yourself. If you tried to do any thing against the white people, they would not treat you as Bonaparte did your namesake, but they'd hang you right off."

"Reckon massa's 'bout right," said the driver. "Massa, please not tell ole massa at de hotel; for he no like to have his niggers talk bout sich tings."

Placed on his guard by this conversation, Bryant was silent the remainder of the way. Toussaint, as he put up his horses, said to the driver of the stage to Tusculum, —

"Queer buckra man dat I druv out to de Sand Hills. He talk 'bout slaves making a resurrection; — tell dis nigger he named after Toussaint, what done make him in Samingo."

"Hush up, you fool; you want ole massa gib you de raw-hide? Your mammy name you Two-cent, cause dat all you bring when dey sell you."

CHAPTER XV.

THE TAVERN AND ITS INMATES.

It had been Bryant's intention, on arriving at Tusculum, to consult Judge Hendrick and the acquaintances of his friend Stevens, before making any attempt to approach either Lizzie or her father. For this purpose he would have preferred not to enter the hotel, and looked round among his fellow-passengers to see if there was any whom he could request to have an eye to the safety of his baggage. But the gentleman was too old and grave for him to take that liberty; the boy was too young; the two ladies were out of the question; and the other passenger had drunk at every resting-place, and mixed his conversation with words as strong as his beverage. Frederick thought too that the endeavor to avoid observation, if too carefully made, might rather tend to attract it, and consequently entered the house with the others, hoping that either he might not meet Witham, or that the slave-dealer would not recognize him.

Witham, however, was within his bar, at the end of

the hall; and as Frederick, after seeing his baggage deposited, turned hastily towards the door, he called to him, —

"Pass the night here, sir? Want a room?"

"Probably," replied Bryant, "but I will not enter my name now. I shall be in again soon. Can you direct me ——"

"Won't take very long, just to write your name. Won't charge you any thing for it, if you go to your friends after all." The last was said with a sneering laugh, for the tavern-keeper supposed the haste of his guest to be prompted by meanness, and set down to the same cause his not calling for any thing at the bar.

Bryant suppressed his irritation, advanced, and silently wrote in the dog's-eared and blotted book, "F. W. Bryant, Irvine, Mass."

The tavern-keeper looked at the name, and then at the writer.

"O, I see why you didn't want to write your name. I remember you well enough."

"We have met before, it is true, Mr. Witham; and I own I did not want to speak with you till I could do so more in private."

"Private! I think it is pretty private, to come into a man's house, mousing round, and not letting one's name be known."

"Mr. Witham, I wish to see you on important business. I came here for the very purpose. I should be happy to speak with you when you are more at leisure. In the mean time, will you please to assign me a room?"

The man glared at him, but Bryant's strong effort at self-control had its reward. The tavern-keeper, surly as he was, could not well refuse the common duty of his business. He marked a number against the name, and Bryant followed the negro, who carried his trunk to the room thus indicated.

"No love lost between you and that young man, Witham," said one of the bystanders. "He spoke soft, but he looked about as cross as you did; and you're not a lamb, nor a dove either."

"Where's he from, Witham?" "What do you know about him?" were the questions of half a dozen others.

"I don't know much about him, and I don't care to know. I've told you, I went to the North first, when I came from England; but I could not stay there; they were too stiff and precise for me. Well, this fellow was one of the stiffest of the whole set, — looked down on a poor man as if he wouldn't touch him with a pair of tongs, — he'd be dreadfully shocked if a man swore, and go into fits if he saw a glass of whiskey."

"Wonder what he comes here for, if he's that sort of fellow," said Jones.

"Wonder if he isn't an abolitionist," said Thompson.

"Them's just the sort to make abolutionists of," said Jones. "These canting, whining people, that think themselves better than others, are always dipping into what don't concern them."

"Here, boy!" said Smith, beckoning to the negro driver of the stage, who was at the other end of the hall. The man came at once, and was interrogated.

"Did that man that went up stairs just now, — the man that made such a fuss with Mr. Witham about putting his name down, — did he have any talk with you as you came up?"

"No, massa; I 'fraid talk with he. I 'fraid."

"What you afraid of, you numskull?"

"Massa, I 'fraid he talk bad to me, as he talk wid Toussaint."

"Talk with who? What was that?" said several voices.

"Massa, you know Toussaint; ole Mas' Tom's boy, down to Royalton?"

"Mas' Tom? O, a boy of Rogers's that keeps the American House there?"

"Yes, massa. Well, Toussaint druv this gen'lman out to de Sand Hills; and he tell me when he come back he was a queer gen'lman. He talk to him 'bout making a rumpus; a 'surrection of de blacks agin de massas. I tell Toussaint, neber let me hear sich anoder word."

"Insurrection!" exclaimed the inquirers, in horror. But Witham, deep as was his dislike of the young lawyer, shrunk from the consequences of the rising excitement. He guessed the object of Bryant's coming; and while determined to baffle it, was not disposed to use or encourage violence against his daughter's lover.

"Nonsense," said he, with an oath. "Don't you know that a nigger's testimony's nothing at all? I don't like this fellow, and I have reason not to like him; but he has other fish to fry than meddling with niggers. He says he comes on business with me, and I reckon you know, boys, that I ain't an abolitionist."

"You — you old nigger-trader!" said Jones, laughing. "But perhaps, fellows, he's come to try and convert old Witham?"

"I thought that prim parson was going to settle that business," said Smith; "that one that came so near mounting a saddle without any girths."

"That trick fell through, though," said Thompson. "And Witham is sore about it; for Colonel Selwyn gave him an awful talking to, when he heard what had been done."

"You brought that on me, boys, and I tell you it was too bad to try such a trick on a man that had brought me a letter. I wasn't quite myself that time. But I tell you, I won't have any more tricks, or any more talk, against people that stay at my house. Mr. Jones, what will you have to drink?"

That magic word led the thoughts of the bar-room loungers away from the subject, which was becoming too serious; and after treating all round, Witham suggested a visit to his bowling-alley, though excusing himself from joining them, on the plea that he could not leave his bar. No sooner were they gone, however, than he left it, and went through the dining-room into a small private parlor, the same which, during the press of commencement week, had been occupied as a bed-room by Stevens and others. He found it now tenanted by his "better half." There could be little question that Mrs. Witham deserved that name.

"Well, Susan," said he, "here's a pretty kettle of fish! Here's Betsy's old flame, that boy that I told you about, come spying round here; and I'll warrant" (we must modify some of his language here and elsewhere) "he's after her again."

"Well, John, and what if he is?" said his wife. "Why not let him take the gal, and be done with it? She keeps a droopin' and a droopin', and there ain't no use of keepin' on her at this rate."

"I should think a gal's own father was good enough for her to live with, any how. Some folks would say that you wanted to get rid of her, because you ain't her own mother; but then you haven't no children of your own, and it seems hard you should go agin the only one I've got."

"O, John, you know it isn't that. I didn't like Betsy at first; I thought she was sort of uppish, and looked down on other folks. But she's been so good and so biddable, it goes to my heart to see her pinin' away."

"I don't see about her being so biddable, when she

keeps a talking to me, as if I was to give account to her of what I do to get her a living."

"But, John, she hasn't said nothin' since you give her that blowin' up, when she took on about your drinking."

"No, I guess she thought it wan't no use, and it wouldn't be. I didn't come away from Old England and New England, both, to be kept down by a little gal in my own house, and told I mustn't drink, nor I mustn't do this, that, and the other — mustn't sell this nigger, and mustn't buy that."

"Well, John, you and she don't get along well together, no how. Now, wouldn't it be better to have a quiet house, and let her go away to the North, if she wants to, along with this young feller."

John took a turn about the room, grumbled a little, and brought out an oath or two, but seemed to be considering, favorably on the whole, the suggestion of his wife, when the sound of loud and angry voices, penetrating the thin partitions of the house, drew his attention. He listened a moment, and then hastily left the room.

The voices which he had heard were those of the men from whom he had parted shortly before, and whom he had supposed safely engaged in the bowling-alley. They seemed in high wrath, and as he entered the bar-room, the first word he heard was "abolitionist," coupled with an adjective more emphatic than courteous.

Frederick Bryant was standing near the stairs, which

he had just descended from the room assigned him. His tall form was proudly erect, and the expression on his face was less of anger or fear than of surprise and contempt. Opposite him were the three bar-room loungers, Smith, Jones, and Thompson, assailing him with their combined abuse. There was something in his aspect that would have daunted them, but they were strong in their numbers, and in Witham's whiskey, to which they had been helping themselves since they returned disappointed from the bowling-alley, having found the door locked.

"So you're not an abolitionist!" said Smith. "O, no! you never done nothing agin the rights of the South! you never set the niggers agin their masters! you double-faced hypocrite, you!"

"I'll tell you, young man, you've come to the wrong place, if you're going to work about in the dark and make mischief between us and the slaves," said Jones. "We have a short way of dealing with such creeping rascals."

"My friends, let us be orderly on this occasion," said Thompson who, though dismissed from the Methodist ministry for intemperance, retained some of the professional forms of speech. "The business we have to do is very solemn, and I could wish it had been introduced by prayer. Our young brother is to be admonished, and if necessary, disciplined ——"

"Disciplined with a cat-o'-nine-tails, and then covered

with a coat of tar and feathers; and I'll see that done, or my name's not Dan Smith."

"Don't come too near," said Frederick; "it might not be safe. I have told you already I am not an abolitionist. If you have any thing to say against me, I am ready to meet your charges before a magistrate."

"Magistrate, indeed! In such a case every man's a magistrate," said Smith. "It's the protection of our lives and our families."

"Our rights as masters, and the safety of our wives and children," added Jones.

"And the poor colored brethren themselves," said Thompson, "whom Providence has placed in our keeping."

"And so," said Smith, "look out, you blasted nigger-stealer. You may look as high and mighty as you please, but if you're found here to-night, you'll have a lesson that'll make you stay north, if ever you get back there."

"Gentlemen," said Witham, as he entered the room, "what's all this about? I can't have my company abused."

"Your company or not, Jack Witham," said Smith, "he's an abolitionist; and we won't have no abolitionists here,—Yankee abolitionists,—no, nor English neither."

"Brother Witham," said Thompson, "the excitement on this occasion is called for. I am a man of peace, but I reckon this is a case for tar and feathers."

"I reckon you're drunk, all of you," said Witham, "and so just clear out of my bar-room."

"Not unless you clear out the Yankee too," said Smith. "Come along, my tall fellow, and let the folks see you outside."

He took rude hold of Bryant's arm; but the latter sternly shook him off, and seized him in turn by the collar. "Out of the door with him," said Witham, grasping Smith on the other side. Together they bore him towards the door, the bully vainly struggling, and uttering threats and curses. Jones and Thompson followed, increasing the tumult with their clamors, but not venturing to rescue their leader. When all were outside the door, Bryant and Witham let go their hold; and Smith, losing his balance, fell prostrate on the floor of the piazza.

"You'll kick up a muss in my bar-room another time!" said Witham, as he turned away. He reëntered the house with Bryant, and locked the door against the vanquished enemy.

"Mr. Bryant," he said, "I did not give you much of a welcome, but I hope you won't mind it. You've got real pluck, and I'm glad of it. Make yourself at home, and pretty soon I'll hear what you've got to say."

CHAPTER XVI.

A STRANGE SCRUPLE.

THE scene which had taken place in Witham's piazza was not entirely without precedent; and there was at first more amusement than pity among those whom the noise drew together, as they saw a drunken brawler borne out of the house which had furnished the means of his intemperance. But when those who had been expelled gave their account of the affair, and declared that Witham was sheltering an agent of the abolitionists, men looked serious. Words were interchanged in low voices; and though the hotel was soon left in silence, there was something in that silence more ominous than the clamor that preceded.

The door had been opened; the usual frequenters of the hotel had assembled, with the exception of the three malecontents, and had gone to dinner at the summons of the bell. The meal had been partaken in silence and haste, but not without many a glance of curiosity or dislike towards Bryant, who filled the seat which Lizzie was accustomed to occupy. Lizzie had been spending the morning with the Wheelers, who, since they had heard of her through Mr. Stevens, had shown her much kindness. They had kept her to dine with them; but, excusing herself after the early meal, she was hastening homeward, when she was joined by Bryant. The path was lonely, and no stranger witnessed Lizzie's start of delighted surprise, or intruded on the greeting of the lovers. The first few moments were of unmixed happiness; but those passed, Lizzie exclaimed, "O, Frederick, I ought not to be so glad. I did not mean that you should have come here."

"No, you did not, you naughty girl; and so you did not let us know where to look for you. But I have found you, in spite of yourself, thank Heaven. O, Lizzie, how anxious we have been for you!"

"I do thank Heaven, indeed, Frederick, to see you once more — once more — once more," she repeated, almost wildly, "and but once more."

"Once more, and forever, Lizzie," said the youth. "I must rescue you from this dismal life that I find you in. If it is a time of trial with you, so much the better time for me to put an end to all trials, as far as a lover or a husband can. But, O Lizzie, why did you not write when you left that place in Alabama? You don't know what a search I have had for you, you little runaway."

"I could not write, Frederick; I thought it was best not. I saw my path was likely to be dark and sad, and it seemed best that I should bear the burden alone."

"I thought as much," said he. "Aunt Richards tried

to make me believe you were indifferent; but I knew your generous heart too well. And you see I have followed you and found you out. Now, the next thing is to return to the North. If you will trust yourself with the lover as far as Royalton, my friend Stevens, there, will give me a still nearer claim."

"O, Frederick, you promised ——"

"Never to propose a runaway match again. And I am not breaking my promise. We will have your father's consent. He received me coldly at first, but now we are on very good terms. And I have more courage to ask than I had before. Then I was only a young law student, with nothing to depend on but a profession I had not tried. Now I have made a beginning, and — and ——"

"You have succeeded, as I knew you would."

"Well, friends have been kind, and flattered me; but, besides that, the death of my grandfather Williams puts me in possession of more property than I shall know what to do with, unless Lizzie comes and helps me."

"Dear Frederick! and all these bright prospects you are willing to darken by marrying a slave-trader's daughter! No, dear, dear, dearest friend, it cannot be; it ought not to be; it must not be."

"Yes, it must be, though. A slave-trader's daughter, indeed! You are the daughter of Richard Livingston, Esq., of Irvine, a man whose honor is above suspicion. As for this man ——"

12 *

"Ah, Frederick, he is my father!"

"O, I have nothing to say against him. You do not know what good friends we are. We have stood side by side, and I am really under very great obligations to him. Besides, I want nothing of him but you; if he offered me any thing else I would not take it. His ways and mine are very different, but I do not doubt we shall get along very well together. Only say, that if he consents, you will not refuse me."

She blushed — faltered — gave him her hand, and said, "Only mind, I cannot go without his consent."

They walked together in happy talk towards her home. Their hopes were high, for every thing seemed favorable to their union; and the loveliness of nature around them, and the luxurious softness of the air on that beautiful afternoon in early autumn, harmonized with every gentle feeling. Witham met them at the door, and expressed neither surprise nor displeasure at seeing them together. They went with him into the private parlor.

"I told you, Mr. Witham," said Bryant, "that I came on business; and you have guessed rightly, that my business concerned your daughter. She is too good a daughter to do any thing without your leave, and I do not ask her to. But I do ask your consent. You know something of my character and standing three years ago. Since then I have entered the profession of the law, and have inherited property enough to make me independent, if I choose, of any profession. I ask your consent to my union with Lizzie."

Witham looked from the speaker to his daughter. She had risen, and with one hand in her lover's, and the other half raised towards himself, looked up in his face with more of affectionate confidence than he had seen in her features since her childhood. The father's heart was touched, and in a softer tone than he had almost ever used, he asked the question, "Betsy, do you want to leave me?"

"Frederick is an old friend," she replied, timidly.

The answer did not quite suit Witham, and his next words showed it. "Well," said he, "I suppose, then, Betsy must go back to her 'old friends' off there at the North, whatever becomes of her father. Perhaps it is best; but I should like to see her sometimes; and you'll let her come and see me? Sometimes, too, I shall go North, as I have done for years."

Bryant looked grave. He had no great wish for intimacy with his intended father-in-law; but he answered, "Certainly. My wife will be at perfect liberty to visit and to receive her friends." He almost spoiled the concession by adding, "I know that Mr. and Mrs. Livingston are anxious to receive her as a daughter, and as we shall live near them ——" He paused, uncertain how to close the sentence.

"As she will live near the Livingstons, her father may as well keep out of the way," said Witham. "But I can tell you Mr. Bryant, a father who brings twenty thousand dollars to his daughter is worth seeing, if he is an old, rough slave-dealer."

"I don't want your money," said Bryant, abruptly. "Excuse me, Mr. Witham, if I seem uncivil. I have abundant means to support my wife, and I ask from you nothing but her. I am willing — more than willing — to take Lizzie without any dowry."

"But I am not willing to let my only child go from me like a beggar. Who should my property go to but her, I wonder? No, Mr. Bryant, you don't like me very well, I know, and I haven't fancied you either; but as Betsy is willing to marry you, she shall bring you what will be worth your having."

"No, I am in earnest, Mr. Witham; I want nothing but Lizzie. And you need not be afraid that she will not be well provided for. Besides what I can do myself, Mr. Livingston, I know ——"

"So you are willing to take Mr. Livingston's money, but not mine!" said Witham. "What is there about my money, that you can't touch it?"

Frederick now saw the dangerous ground that he was on; but he was too conscientious to conceal the nature of his scruple.

"You know," said he, "our feeling at the North with regard to slavery. I share in those feelings; and while I do not undertake to dictate to others what they should do, I am resolved never to own a slave, or any property that has any thing to do with slavery."

"Very particular, you are, young man," said Witham, with a sarcastic laugh. "A good many of your northern folks have no objection at all to a southern wife, with a good large plantation and half a hundred niggers. But I have no plantation, and not a nigger of mine shall trouble you. All I have, except what's about the house, and a few that a partner of mine is off with to sell in Texas, — all except them is in good sound stock of the Xenophon Bank, and Betsy shall have ten thousand of it when she's married, and at least ten thousand more when I give up the ship. Let's see what you say to that, my boy!"

"I say as before, sir," said Bryant. "All I ask of you is this dear girl. I cannot accept of any property that has been made by slave-trading."

"Then, by Heaven, you had better look for some man's daughter that you can ask for without insulting him to his face. Betsy can find enough to be glad to take her and her money too, without crying after a born fool of an abolitionist. No, no, Betsy, don't cling to me, nor kneel, nor cry, nor say a word for him. You've seen the last of him, or my name's not John Witham. And as for you, sir, you'd better be quick and leave the place before the people are after you, for there's a breeze stirring already, or, if there isn't, there soon will be. Clear out from my house, and if ever you enter it again, the chance will be you'll get the welcome of a pistol ball."

Bryant confronted the angry man with aspect not less determined than his own. "Spare your threats, sir," he said. "They will have no power with me. I have refused to defile my hands with your ill-gotten gold, and I would not unsay that refusal, though it would gain me the treasure I seek beyond all else in life. I will not intrude further in your family; but no threats shall prevent me from watching for Lizzie's good. If she ever wants a friend, she will know on whom to call; and if she suffers from your heartless tyranny, you too, sir, shall find that she has a defender near." Regardless of Witham's presence, he stooped down and kissed the almost fainting girl; then turned, and passed from the room with a lofty tread.

He left the house, and walked rapidly along the path at its side, which he had so recently trodden with Lizzie, full of the high hopes, which were now again crushed to the earth. Having gone some distance, he turned towards the hotel, then, reaching it, turned again, when the thought struck him through the tumult of his feelings, what course he should next pursue. He now remembered that he had not yet called on his old friend Judge Hendrick, nor delivered the letters of introduction to others, with which Stevens had furnished him; and as he considered the circumstances in which he was placed, he saw the importance of securing the interest of those who might assist him in the designs which his mind began to revolve. These were indefinite, or, when they assumed a distinct form, they appeared extravagant and impossible. He was resolved to watch over Lizzie's safety and happiness; but would it contribute to either for him to linger as an idler in the village where she dwelt, and where, after what had passed, he could not expect to be permitted to visit her? He had been authorized by Mr. and Mrs. Livingston to urge on Witham that he should send his daughter to them for a visit, if not for permanent residence; but in his eagerness for the accomplishment of his own wishes, he had omitted all mention of this proposal, and neither pride nor prudence sanctioned a recurrence to it now. Should he write to Mr. Livingston, and suggest to him to apply to Witham for that purpose? He felt that the scene of the last hour had left little hope for the success of such an application, even if made by Lizzie's former protectors; and his mind revolted at the thought of requesting his honored friends to make overtures to the slave-trader. Uncertain of his course, he was only firmly resolved not to abandon the protection of the innocent and unhappy, nor to resign the hope of union with one, of whose affection for himself he was fully assured. Perhaps, if he could not make friends in Tusculum, they could give him advice or aid. With this thought, he left the hotel, — where he felt that he was remaining only by the sufferance of the man with whom he had quarrelled, — and inquired the way to Judge Hendrick's.

His cordial reception by the judge encouraged him to

enter, with brief preface, on the story of his visit to Tusculum, its cause, and its ill success. The judge shook his head at the idea of his gentlemanly visitor's seeking a union with the daughter of the notorious Witham. "My dear sir," said he, "I have no doubt you feel warmly, as young men always do; but you must let me take the cool view of an older person. Give up this undertaking. The connection is one that would always be an embarrassment to you. Even we, who hold slaves, consider the business this man follows as disreputable; and how would it appear in your section of the country, where the prejudice is so strong against our whole system? If she would run away with you indeed, — those things take place here pretty often, and a man is not thought less of for having married in that way, — I should think, with such a father, she would be glad to; and brought up away from him, too."

"She will not consent to that, sir; and I honor her scruples too much to urge her. In fact, I have promised never to propose it again."

"That is certainly in her favor; rather over-scrupulous, though; unless, indeed, there is a view of it which may not be pleasing, but ought to be considered. Some would say, the love cannot be very deep that objects to such a trial under such circumstances."

"O, I have no doubt on that score. I think, too, that besides her sense of natural and religious duty, she has thought much of a charge given her by her mother, just before she died, to obey her father, and stay with him if he should ever return."

"Well, whatever the reason, she has made her choice. She will stay with her father, and she will not go with you. What more have you to say? You cannot marry a lady in spite of her own will."

"But she consented, if his sanction could be obtained; and we almost had it, when an unlucky circumstance brought us to high words, and we parted."

"So you said; but you did not name the circumstance. Some years hence, perhaps, you may regard it as a fortunate interruption."

"The subject we got on was that of slavery."

"Slavery! I wish those busybodies would let slavery alone. But what had slavery to do with it? Did Witham want you to live here, and go into the business with him?"

"Not quite so bad as that, sir; he only began telling what he could give his daughter; and I declined touching his property, knowing how it had been gained."

"You did, indeed! Then you had no view to the old man's money-bags. Strange! The first instance that ever I knew of a man quarrelling with his future father-in-law, or with any one else, for giving him too much money. If that is all, it seems to me the difficulty might be got over. It is not generally very hard to persuade people to keep their money."

"I am afraid, sir, the breach is irreconcilable. Certainly I would never accept a dollar from him."

"Your views seem rather romantic. There are many from the North who like our southern beauties all the better for the negroes they own."

"Perhaps so, sir; but they remain here, and become southern in their feelings. Or, if not, at least their feelings and mine are different. I am to live at the North. I am in a profession which often leads to public life. This subject of slavery is exciting more and more attention; and whichever side I take, it must not be said that I am bribed with a slave-trader's money, nor that I am base enough to oppose the system, and yet receive its wages."

"You're a little of a fanatic, but I don't like you the worse for it. You go according to the rules and feelings of your state, as I go for mine. But as for your affair, if you won't take my advice and give it up, the best thing you can do is to stay here a while, and see if any change takes place in old Witham's feelings. You cannot properly stay at his house, of course; so you must be my guest. Take tea with us now, and I will send one of my people to the hotel for your baggage."

The offer was, after some hesitation, gratefully accepted. Judge Hendrick led his guest into another room, and introduced him to his family. The evening meal was served, and Bryant found his depression cheered by the intelligence and refinement of the circle around, when a servant entered the room and handed him a note. He opened it, and read as follows: —

"There is a crowd around the house, threatening vengeance against you as an abolitionist. They will soon learn where you have gone. Escape while you have time. E. W."

"I must leave here at once, Judge Hendrick, or I may bring trouble upon you," said Bryant, showing the note to his entertainer.

"It may be the best course, indeed," said the judge — "not for my sake, but your own. I will send Henry with you to Professor Wheeler's. It will hardly be suspected that you have gone there; and if matters look serious, I will send a saddle horse, with which I advise you to make your way out of this neighborhood at once."

"Thanks for your great kindness," said the young man; "but there will be, I trust, no occasion for it. I will return to the hotel."

"You must not think of such a thing, Mr. Bryant," said Mrs. Hendrick. "You would be rushing into a den of wild beasts."

"I will not own myself guilty by running away," said Bryant, proudly. "I have done nothing, and intended nothing, against the peace or the institutions of this section. I will meet those that charge me with it. I have a good deal of confidence in the justice of the people, if properly appealed to; and if danger comes, I had rather die standing than running. Besides, Mr. Witham's house is endangered on my account, and there is at least one there whose safety I must provide for."

"I am not sure but Mr. Bryant is right," said the judge. "The attempt to escape might fail, from his want of knowledge of the country; and I think, if I go with him, I have influence enough to protect him from ill treatment."

Bryant objected to his host's exposing himself; and Mrs. Hendrick, with trembling voice, tried to dissuade her husband; but the judge was not to be deterred from fulfilling the duty of hospitality. He laughed at his wife's fears, asking her if she thought he was not pretty well known in Tusculum; and after he had given some directions to a servant, the two gentlemen left the house arm in arm, and walked rapidly towards the hotel, around which they soon saw the gathered crowd, and heard the cries that bore witness to their excitement.

CHAPTER XVII.

THE MOB.

THE account which the stage-driver had given to the bar-room loungers, of Bryant's conversation with the negro Toussaint, had not fallen on inattentive ears. The men who heard it, having little to do but to drink, and occasionally to gamble or fight, naturally employed the time which their own affairs did not demand in attending to those of their neighbors; and as soon as they had parted from Witham, they proceeded to discuss, with no little vehemence, the purposes and the abolition propensities of Witham's new guest. It was not strange that they should connect his arrival with Witham's daughter; and as Smith, the leading spirit among them, had already, in his own mind, aspired to her hand, he was the less disposed to see the prize conferred on a stranger and an abolitionist. When, therefore, he had returned from the bowling-alley to the bar-room, and finding it unoccupied, had helped himself and his companions liberally to Witham's liquor, the entrance of Bryant at once prompted his rude attack; and, when this had led to his own expulsion from the house, he and his associates were neither scrupulous nor idle in spreading the intelligence that there was an abolition agent at the Eagle Hotel, and that the landlord had taken his part against some public-spirited gentlemen who were disposed to call him to account. The better class of citizens, opposed as they were to abolitionism, paid little regard to statements from such a source; but there were enough of the idle, the ignorant, and the violent to spread the excitement, and others joined the gathering crowd through mere curiosity.

Thus it was that in front of the hotel there was now assembled a crowd of men and boys, blending in rude chorus their various cries, "State Rights!" "Southern Rights!" "Nullification!" "Down with the Yankees!" and "Down with the Abolitionists!" Smith and his two companions, Jones and Thompson, with some others, were in consultation on the piazza, while at the windows appeared the faces of the servants of the house. Witham advanced from his bar, himself somewhat excited with liquor, and seeing no better way of conciliating the crowd than to invite them to share the same excitement.

"Ask Mr. Thompson and Mr. Jones to walk in and take some refreshment, Cato," said he. "There's that fellow Smith again!—his impudence! Mr. Wilkins, Mr. Jameson, walk in, gentlemen. What will you have to drink, gentlemen? Walk in, and make yourselves at home."

The leaders of the mob approached, without replying to his invitation; and Thompson, who thought he had the gift of eloquence, pressing before the rest, endeavored to announce their business.

"Mr. Witham, we are a committee of the free and — and — free and patriotic citizens of Tusculum, assembled on this occasion, — I repeat, on this occasion ——"

"Witham," broke in Smith, "there's a —— abolitionist in the house, and we are going to tar and feather him."

"Hang him," cried another voice — "come here to set the niggers to cutting our throats! Hanging's too good for him."

"Tar and cotton him," said a student from the college, more facetiously, perhaps, more mercifully inclined. "Think, fellows, what a pretty bird he will be, with cotton for feathers; — so downy."

"Tar and cotton, tar and cotton!" cried several voices.

"With a good whipping to begin with," said Smith. "Witham, where's your raw-hide?" — that name being given to a certain long, twisted instrument of correction.

"Let's have a tar-kettle," cried Jones. "Here, you boys, Zeke and Samson, leave your staring out of that window, and bestir yourselves. Run over to old Moody's, and tell him his tar-kettle's wanted for the public service."

"And, Scip, you nigger," said Smith, "off to Peters's warehouse, and get some cotton."

"Mas' Peters' wa'house done lock up for de night," said Scip.

"Some of you go, boys, and break the gate open," said Jones. "No bales come in yet, but you'll find waste enough lying about."

"But where's the fellow himself?" cried Smith. "Witham, what have you done with him? We demand to see the man that's been staying here to-day, and talking abolitionism round among our niggers." Smith had never owned a negro, or any thing else, worth a five dollar bill.

"I've nothing to say to you, Dan Smith. I shall have something to say, by and by, to your sorrow. If any *gentleman* has any thing to say to me, I'm ready to hear him, and give him a civil answer; but I tell you, Dan Smith, the less words from you to me the better."

"Hurrah for Jack Witham! A nigger-dealer turned abolitionist! But that's all you could expect in a —— Englishman. I say, boys, if Witham don't give him up, let's burn the house down."

"Hang the Yankee and the Englishman both," cried another voice.

"Brethren," said Thompson, — "gentlemen, I mean, — let us act as orderly citizens on this occasion. We represent the dignity of the chivalrous South. Let us obtain an interview with this suspected person, and, having brought home to him a statement of the enormity of the crimes laid to his charge, crimes which, rousing the feeling of indignation in the breast of this entire community, alarming all classes for the safety of our peculiar institutions, our wives, our children, and our — our — our sacred honor, have brought us together on this occasion, in rightful vindication —— "

" Let's have him here, and set Thompson to talk at him," said Jones.

" That would be some punishment in itself," said the facetious and merciful student.

" There's Judge Hendrick coming, boys ! " cried one, who stood near the end of the piazza. " There's the judge coming, and somebody with him. Wonder what the old judge will think of all this ! "

" Think ? " said Smith. " If he don't think it right to stand up for the institutions of the South, I reckon he won't get many votes when he's up for the judgeship next time."

" Who's that with him ? " cried several at once.

" I'll be —— if it isn't that man himself that we are after," said Jones.

" Is it ? " said the student. " Abolitionist or not, he has a good deal of pluck."

The judge and his companion approached, the crowd making way for them, and ascended the steps amid a general silence. The judge himself was the first to break it.

" Mr. Witham," said he, " what is the meaning of this crowd? Is any thing unusual going on in your house that calls so many of our fellow-citizens together around it?"

"The folks have come together, judge, out of some foolery that Dan Smith has put in their heads. But walk in, walk in, judge. Not you, though, Mr. Bryant, or whatever your name is. I don't want you in my house; and you may just take your things and find lodgings elsewhere, if you can get any."

"I do not wish to enter your house at present, Mr. Witham. I came back on purpose to talk with these gentlemen, who, I understood, were desirous to speak to me. Gentlemen, my name is Frederick Bryant, a stranger, who arrived in Tusculum this morning. I understand you have business with me."

"Our business, Mr. Bryant," began Thompson, "is — is of a serious kind. The circumstances under which we are assembled, on this occasion, are connected with those rights of freedom, and those noble though peculiar institutions, in defence of which our revolutionary fathers ——"

"We hear, Mr. Bryant," said Smith, "that you are a —— abolitionist; you've been talking abolitionism to our niggers, stirring them up to insurrection; and you've been talking abolitionism to Witham here; and we've made up our minds to give you a hundred lashes, and a coat of tar and cotton, and send you out of the state about the quickest. So lose no time talking, but off with your coat."

"Keep your distance, scoundrel," said Bryant. "Gentlemen," he added, raising his voice till its powerful tones rang to the remotest of the crowd, "is it possible you are about to commit an outrage on a stranger without letting him hear the evidence on which he is accused, or have an opportunity to defend himself? I have been in this town little more than six hours. What have I done in that short time to deserve such a punishment as that with which this man threatens me? I have not spoken to a single negro in the place, unless it was to give some direction about my baggage, or to inquire the way; and, if you have heard any thing of a conversation elsewhere, it must have been very much misrepresented, to make any harm out of it. Those I have spoken with here have been principally Mr. Witham and Judge Hendrick; and I ask any man of common sense if I should have been likely to select them as subjects for the infusion of abolition sentiments. Mr. Witham you know. I shall say little of him, for he and I do not agree. Judge Hendrick is your respected fellow-townsman, a Southerner by birth, and one who would never countenance any thing against the peace of the community in which he resides. I appeal to him to say, if I have, to his knowledge, advocated insurrection, or said or done any thing, which I had not, as a free but peaceful citizen, a right to say or do."

"And I," said the judge, "testify most fully and most willingly in favor of Mr. Bryant. I am well acquainted with his friends, and have known himself from his boyhood; and his purpose in visiting Tusculum I know to be a legal and proper one. His views on some subjects may be different from ours; but I am fully assured that he has not, since he has been here, said or done any thing against the peace of the community, and convinced that he has no desire to say or do any thing of the kind."

"Good!" exclaimed the student. "We shall not see our downy bird this time. And, in truth, I had rather see him in his black broadcloth than in Dan Smith's fancy dress." Many of the crowd seemed of the same opinion; numbers left it, and took the way to their homes. But the leaders seemed not yet satisfied.

"Judge Hendrick," said Mr. Thompson, "the interests involved in the gathering of this occasion are too important to be left undefended, or any injury to them unvindicated and unavenged. Notwithstanding the manner in which your friend — if it is not disrespectful to you, sir, to speak of an abolitionist as your friend — has spoken on this occasion ——"

"I agree fully with all that Mr. Thompson has said," broke in Jones. "If he is an abolitionist, he can't stay here. As Judge Hendrick stands up for him, we may let him off, I suppose, without the flogging and the tar-kettle, provided we are assured that he will leave the state at once."

"I shall leave the state," said Bryant, "when it suits my own convenience."

"Bravely, but rather rashly said," remarked the

judge. "Mr. Bryant, gentlemen, is a man of courage, and you will not think the worse of him for that. But I agree with you, he had better leave the city. His business here is, I understand, in great part transacted; and in what remains of it, he can act through letters. I pledge myself then, gentlemen, that he will leave the city early to-morrow morning. As to his leaving the state, I do not think, gentlemen, that it is our business to enforce that; but I willingly receive his assurance that he will do so as soon as may be, consistently with his own convenience."

"That's putting the thing rather differently," said the student. "Mr. Bryant, I will stand by you, and, if any one here would harm a hair of your head, he will have to do with Ned Elmsley and a few college lads that go with him sometimes. Logomachians, to the rescue!" he cried; and the air rang with a sudden response in the same words, while numbers of the students forced their way through the crowd, and gathered at the foot of the piazza steps.

"Fellow-citizens," said Thompson, "we are assembled on this occasion to do justice on a person accused of incendiary conduct. Mr. Elmsley, and you gentlemen of the college, you will not surely protect such a person!"

"Drive the college boys home to their mothers," cried Smith. "Down with the abolitionist!" He rushed forward to strike at Bryant, but was intercepted by Elmsley. As the partisans on either side crowded round, leaving a space about the door, the judge drew Bryant within it, and shut and locked it. It was done so suddenly, that the young man scarce understood the action; but instantly recovering himself, he exclaimed, "I must not leave my defender at the mercy of that crowd," and attempted to unfasten the door.

"Come," said the judge, "don't be crazy. You will do more harm than good by staying. The college boys will take care of their comrade; and all will be safe, if you are only out of the way."

Bryant saw the necessity of yielding, and followed the judge as he went quickly through the house. As they passed through the dining-room, the door of the private parlor was open, and they saw Witham standing before a desk, from which he was taking articles of value to secure them from the mob.

Most southern dwellings, whether large or small, consist of two separate portions; one for the white members of the family, and one for the colored. In the most recent clearing of the interior settlements, the log-cabins are in pairs, one square room being provided for the accommodation of the ruling race, and another for their dependants. If these are connected by a roof, covering the space between, that space answers the purposes of piazza, wash-room, and dining-room. The city mansion has no slaves lodged, and no cooking done, within its proper precincts; but beyond a court in its rear is a building comprising the kitchen and the servants' rooms.

In such a building the wife and daughter of Witham had taken refuge, when the shouts and menaces of the crowd were heard in front of the hotel. Lizzie, relieved, in part, of anxiety on Bryant's account, by learning from old Cato that he had gone to Judge Hendrick's, had sent to him thither her few lines of timely warning; and now endeavored to still the beating of her own heart by doing what she could to cheer her step-mother.

" O," said Mrs. Witham, " Betsy, what will become of us? There's father been as mad as a March hare with Dan Smith, and turned him out of the house, and now, here's Smith come back, and all the fellows with him, a tearin' and a ragin'! And it's all along of that man of yourn. Why couldn't he let you alone, now you was with us, and had done with him and all his folks? But he must be runnin' after you, and puttin' us all to our wit's end. It's a bad thing, a very bad thing, Betsy, to have a lot of young men a danglin' after you."

" O, if I was sure that Frederick was safe out of the way!" said Lizzie. "Let him be once gone, once safe, safe home, and no more young men shall give you trouble on my account."

" Why, Betsy, child, don't cry. I hope your man will get away safe; and some time or 'nother all will come right. What on airth was it he and father fell out about? Something of his abolution, I reckon. But abolution or not, he's a fine, handsome feller, and I hope he'll be yourn yet."

"No," said the daughter; "no: the sooner I dismiss that fancy, the better. I have brought him nothing but trouble; and now his coming to me here has brought him danger, and what people call disgrace. I hear his pure name coupled with the charge of being a base incendiary. O, if he quits this place, let him never come near the slave-dealer's daughter again. Heaven will help me to bear my burden alone, and may his course be as happy as it will always be noble."

"Never happy, unless you share it, dearest," said a voice outside the window against which she leaned. Bryant, after passing through the house, had been left by the judge, while he went to see if his servant was ready with the horse which he had directed him to bring, in case a quick retreat should be necessary.

"Frederick! You here?" said Lizzie. "O, why did you come back? Did you not get my note?"

"I had it, and I shall always keep it as a dear memorial of your care for me; but I felt that I ought to be here, and face the danger. Now I have faced it, I will be as prudent as my friends desire. Only, are you in safety? Can I do any thing to protect or serve you?"

"No, Frederick, I am where I ought to be; and, if I have any trials, I am getting used to them. You cannot help any one here; indeed, your presence may be a source of danger to my father. My love to dear father and mother at Irvine, and Heaven's blessing go with you."

The shouts which had been heard indistinctly, as their sound came from the front of the house, now burst forth nearer and louder. Some, finding the door locked against them, had entered the house through the windows from the piazza; others were coming round, outside of the building.

"One parting kiss, my heart's best love," said Frederick. "Life together on earth, if it be Heaven's will; if not, hereafter."

"Hereafter, forever," said she, as she stooped towards him. The noise increased. "Now fly," she exclaimed, as she saw her father at the opposite door.

Witham, after taking the property and papers he wished to secure, had seized a pistol to protect himself and what he had about him from possible danger on that wild night, and was now hastening to join his wife and child, and escape with them from the building, which some of the rioters had threatened to burn. He witnessed the kiss of parting between his daughter and the man whose coming had brought this trouble on his house, the man who despised his trade, and had scorned his offered gold. Many a deed of blood has been committed because the instrument was at hand, when a moment's thought would have prevented it. Witham uttered a deep curse, raised his pistol, and fired. At that moment, a man rushed into the court from the right, with the cry, "Down with the Yankee incendiary!" met Witham's bullet, and fell. Bryant reached the gate on the left, ran past the private jail, and found at the stables Judge Hendrick and his servant.

"Take this horse, and ride for your life," cried the judge. "The south road leads to Palmetto, where you will meet a stage. O, don't spend time in thanking me," — as Bryant began, — "and as to payment, only write me how you get along."

CHAPTER XVIII.

COUNTRY LIVING AND RELIGION.

FREDERICK BRYANT waited no longer. With a hasty grasp of the hand of his noble friend, he sprung into the saddle. The horse, excited by the shouts and the flashing lights that began to appear, needed no spur. The rider's mind was too full of other thoughts to take in the direction which had been given for his course; and it was not until the animal was turning up the avenue to Judge Hendrick's house, that Bryant recalled the necessity of a decision. Quickly checking the creature's hopes of his familiar stable, he pursued the road, indifferent whither it led him, and chafing at the necessity which compelled his flight. It galled his spirit that he should be obliged to fly before such unworthy foes. How, he thought, would his conduct appear to the young man who had so bravely taken his part? And what might happen, in the excitement of that hour, to endanger her he loved? More than once the thought arose of returning, and braving every danger, rather than desert his generous defender and the unfortunate object of his attachment. But reason told him that to both of these his absence would be more likely to bring safety than his presence. He continued on his way, therefore, though with reduced speed. He knew not whither he was going, and he cared not. Love and honor, he bitterly thought, lay behind him; it was cold duty alone that beckoned him on. If pursued, he would struggle, as well as an unarmed man could, against being captured; and that struggle might win for him at least a pistol-ball, instead of the disgraceful treatment with which he had been threatened, or the felon's death, which would more probably be his doom, if he now fell into the hands of the infuriated crowd.

But there was no thought of pursuing him. The feelings of the people were now turned towards another object. Death, the solemn messenger from another world, had entered the scene of their excitement, and all stood in awe before him. Judge Hendrick, as he walked towards his home, was surprised at the suddenness with which the shouts of the mob died away.

Witham had been found, by those who entered the court, standing as if spell-bound, with the pistol in his hand, and looking with an expression of horror upon the man who lay on the ground before him. Turning from the vain attempt to find signs of life in Smith, they fiercely interrogated the tavern-keeper, but could get no answer from him. He suffered the pistol to be taken from his hand; and it was passed from one to another, each one noticing the marks of its recent use. Screams from the servants' building, at first scarcely heard in the greater interest of the scene before them, now drew the attention of all. Jones tried the door, but found it locked; and as he shook it to obtain entrance, a voice called to him, "Please to don't, massa. Young missis most dead, and ole missis takin' on; please go 'way now, please go 'way."

"Shut up about your old missis and young missis," replied Jones. "Here, some of you, come out and take care of poor Smith."

"He's past taking care of," said Thompson, bending over his former companion with real feeling. "Well, it's an awful thing to go so suddenly."

"Why don't you secure the murderer?" said one of the crowd.

"Send for the coroner," cried another.

Both suggestions were immediately acted on. Several voices at once told Witham that he must consider himself a prisoner; and without a word of remonstrance or acquiescence, he went, with those who had taken his capture upon themselves, into the inner room, and sat down near the desk, from which, not half an hour before, he had taken the fatal pistol. Others went in search of the coroner, and, after some delay, returned with that officer. He, however, decided to postpone his inquest to the following day. Some needful directions were now given, and the hotel was left in charge of a young man who was Witham's assistant in his bar. In one room lay the body of the slain man, watched over by those who had been the partners of his dissipation, but whose feelings now, touched by the suddenness of his death, raised them for a time to a better character. The wretched man who had so strangely stained his hands in blood, cowered in another room, under the guard of two who had volunteered to keep watch over him; and his mourning wife and daughter had been left to the care of the household slaves.

The college clock had struck twelve, when the sentinel, who now alone guarded Witham's sleepless and speechless rest, — for the other had lain down to sleep, intending to take his turn in watching afterwards, — heard a gentle tap upon the door, and, opening it, saw a pale girl with a lamp in her hand.

"May I speak with my father, Mr. Anderson?" she inquired.

"I am sorry to refuse you, Miss Witham," said the guard, "but my orders were to let no one see him. It is late, too, and you have had an exciting time; you had better go to bed."

"I only want to see how he is, and speak a word of comfort to him."

The guard glanced towards his prisoner, and thought it might be well if any thing could rouse him from that hopeless trance, and enable him to give some account of what had happened. He replied, therefore, "Come in, then; but I must hear what you say together."

Lizzie looked deprecatingly, but saw it was in vain to object to this condition. She advanced gently into the room, knelt down near her father, and took his hand in hers. Its trembling was the only sign that he was aware of her presence.

"Father," she began, "dear father, you will be glad to hear that mother is better. She has been quite ill with hysterics, but is now asleep."

A sigh was the only answer.

"I have not been well myself,—that is, I believe I fainted; but I am well now,—that is, better."

It was not now a sigh, but a groan.

"Father,"—and she hesitated,—"do not trouble yourself about what you said to me. I know that it cannot be; it ought not to be; I will try to feel right about it. Father, can you forgive me all the trouble I have brought on you?"

The strong man groaned again, then threw his arms around her, laid his head on her fair young neck, and burst into tears.

But had she then forgotten her lover, that she could pass so lightly the remembrance that her father's hand had been raised against his life? No; her fainting had prevented an accurate knowledge of what had happened. Witham conjectured at once that she knew not with what intent he had fired the pistol; and he resolved that, as far as depended on him, she should never know.

Meantime, Frederick Bryant had pursued the road which chance had given him, till night had gathered round; and the moon soon rising, he continued to advance, in hope of reaching some village, whose tavern would afford the needed rest for himself and his horse. But villages in the Southern States are of rare occurrence, except those of the slaves, which exist on every large plantation; and though in the upper country the slaves are fewer in proportion than on the seaboard, the cabins of the poorer white inhabitants are not usually found together, but widely scattered. At length, about midnight, fatigue, and the failure to find a better resting-place, induced the young man to stop before a log-cabin, which stood, with its rough plank door and unglazed window, in a recent clearing by the road-side. His knock and call were answered by a man who, though evidently ill pleased at his coming so late, yet did not refuse to receive him, and soon came out to take care of the stranger's horse. The rough building had but one large room, in three corners of which were beds, completely shrouded from view by chintz curtains. In one of these his host found room for Bryant, disturbing for a moment the sound sleep of the two boys that occupied it already. He threw himself on his scanty portion of the hard couch, dressed as he was; and, before long, fatigue of body and of mind made it as easy to him as ever had been the best accommodations of his distant home.

He was awakened in the morning by the sound of voices, and of persons in motion, though his young bed-fellows still slept, and, looking forth, discovered that the hive was both populous and busy. The mother of the family and her two girls were astir; and his host was already abroad at work. Quickly rising, he went out, and found means for a simple toilet in the form of a tin basin near a spring. A little way off, he saw his entertainer, and accosted him with, "A pleasant morning, my friend."

"Yes, sir," said the man, "though I don't like the looks of that cloud. It's larger than the one that Elijah saw, already, for that was no bigger than a man's hand; and I shouldn't wonder if this one grew as fast, and came down as heavy."

"I must take my chance of it, however. I judge, from the looks of your clearing here, that you have not lived here long."

"No, sir; I came from the Old North State."

"What's that? New Hampshire, Vermont, or Maine?"

"Not quite so far," said the man, with a smile; "we call North Ca'lina the Old North State; and a good, steady old state it is; not so spry and restless as South Ca'lina, and not troubled with quite so many lazy, worthless slaves."

"But though you like it so well, you came away from it."

"Yes, I thought I'd come and try the gold region, and so I settled there away under Mount Yonah; but I didn't like the company, and so I came here. I said to them, as Abraham said to Lot, 'If you will go to the east I will go to the west.'"

"Why, what was the matter with the company?"

"Too much drinking and gambling for my taste. The first settlers there were a hard set. They would work all day to dig and wash a little gold-dust, and spend the night in gambling it away. And then came another set, that brought in lots of slaves; and I want to bring up my boys to work, not to be ashamed of it, and leave all work to the niggers."

"I should think, then, you would have gone farther off, to the free states."

"No, sir; I'm a southern man, any how. There's plenty of room round here; and then there's some dear brethren that I like to be near."

"Brethren?"

"Yes, brethren in religion, I mean. I'm what they call a Christian."

"Christian! I hope we all are Christians."

"Well, I wish we all were, I'm sure. But there's a set of us people round here, and more off at the West, that don't believe in having any name of a sect, but Christian; and I'm one of them."

"Indeed! Do you preach among them?"

"Sometimes I do; but I'm not a regular preacher. You see, I have my family and my little place here to take care of, and I can't spare time to ride round on a circuit. I'm afraid I shan't be able even to go to the camp-meeting to-day, over at Henderson; but I expect to be there to-morrow, and take the folks with me. But there's wife blowing the horn for us to come in to breakfast."

The breakfast, neat, simple, and substantial, was prefaced by a prayer from the farmer preacher; and after the refreshment Bryant departed, his host receiving, as a matter of course, the payment which he offered for his entertainment.

"I think you'd better not travel, with that cloud over you," said he; "but if you must go, and mean to keep on this road, it will lead you directly to Henderson, where our camp-meeting is; and if you stop there, and see Colonel Freeman,—he's one of the deacons, and lives close by the camp-ground,—you can tell him that you saw brother Sheridan, and that he sent him his love, and hopes to be there to-morrow, and to receive a blessing."

Parting with the worthy settler, Bryant pursued his way. What should be his ultimate course he was yet uncertain; but for the present, the road that led most directly from Tusculum seemed the safest. He had not travelled far, however, when the warning of his host proved to have been correctly given. Rain began to fall, at first in scattered drops, then in an increasing shower, and finally in a steady, unceasing deluge. Wet to the skin, he rode on, mile after mile, without seeing any place of shelter. At length a building near the road-side, reminding him in its appearance of a northern country school-house, gave some promise; and his horse, less from the guiding rein than his own choice, turned with hasty feet toward the adjoining shed. Bryant dismounted, and knocked in vain at the door. He then tried to open it; but it was locked, and the shutters, which covered the apertures for light, were fastened within. It was, in fact, a country church; but supposing it to be a dwelling, he concluded that its occupants had gone to the neighboring meeting, and, after allowing his horse a little time to rest, continued his journey through the rain.

The middle of the day brought him to the camping ground. The road through the woods suddenly expanded, and he saw before him what seemed a village; for the log-houses differed but little from those which he had seen before as permanent dwellings. In the centre of the wide space which these huts surrounded, were rows of benches, fronting a stand for preaching, — but stand and benches were alike unoccupied; while the worshippers were conducting their services under shelter from the still unabated rain. From one of the huts Bryant caught the chorus of a hymn, sung by numerous voices: —

> "Brethren, pray, and holy manna
> Shall come streaming all around."

Some, whose duty it was to receive visitors to the religious encampment, came forth at the sound of his horse's feet, and welcomed him with compassion for his dripping condition. His inquiry for Colonel Freeman, and his mention of the name of his entertainer of last night, made his reception still more cordial; and though he made haste to explain that he was only a passing traveller, and not of their sect, he lost nothing by his sincerity. He was at once ushered to Colonel Freeman's, a large and plain, though well-built house, near the camp-ground, where he was supplied with dry clothing, and soon called to meet the colonel and a large company at an abundant meal.

It was impossible for him to continue his journey that day, had he been more disposed than he was to refuse the hospitality which urged his remaining. After dinner, therefore, he went out with his entertainer, and visited one of the booths, where, when they arrived, religious services had already been resumed. They were conducted in an earnest though simple manner; and if the language of some uneducated preacher would at times excite a smile, the sentiments expressed were such as every Christian heart could unite in. There were a few slaves present, the servants of Colonel Freeman, and of others in the neighborhood; but they were present as fellow-worshippers, and were addressed by one of the speakers with kind words, and in a manner which showed that the recognition of spiritual fraternity was not in words alone. There seemed to be no regular order of services in the meeting, — prayer, singing, and exhortation succeeding each other, at the option of those who were prepared to lead in either. Once, when a brother, having exhausted his stock of thoughts, was continuing his address in wearisome repetition, Bryant was surprised and amused at the sudden raising of a psalm tune by another preacher; the audience joined in the singing, and the speaker stopped without any appearance of irritation.

The rain had ceased; and, after the evening meal, the company from all the booths gathered in the central enclosure. Several preachers, in turn, occupied the stand; and the religious feeling, strengthened by the sympathy of numbers, displayed itself in fervent addresses, prayers, and singing, and in the tears on many cheeks. Bryant himself was deeply moved. The last night, he had yielded to despondency, so far as to forget that providential care which watches constantly over the course of virtue. Now, the affectionate pleadings of these uncultivated speakers, and the deep emotion of their rustic audience, at once reproved his unbelief, and softened his heart to acknowledge and to trust in the Friend who is ever near.

After the meeting, he sought a private interview with his hospitable entertainer, and told him frankly of his imprudent conversation with a slave, of the suspicion which had consequently fallen upon him, and of the aid which Judge Hendrick had given him for leaving Tusculum. He inquired if he could find the means of sending back to the judge his horse, and of purchasing another, or otherwise continuing his journey. There was something in Bryant's open manliness which always won the hearts of those who, like himself, were true; and Colonel Freeman readily undertook to aid his stranger guest in what he wished to accomplish. Arrangements were made the next morning for sending the horse to Tusculum; and Bryant, in his letter of thanks to Judge Hendrick, gave directions for forwarding to New York the baggage he had left at the hotel, and requested intelligence of occurrences since his departure. He enclosed a bank note to cover expenses, requesting his friend to use what might remain of it for some purchase which should preserve the memory of one who owed so much to his generous protection. The colonel furnished Bryant, on moderate terms, with another horse, shook him cordially by the hand, and saw him depart on the road to Knoxville, Tennessee.

CHAPTER XIX.

AN INDIAN CHIEF AND A STRAY POET.

THE course which our traveller was now directed to pursue, lay somewhat west of that which his friend Stevens had taken, when continuing his summer ramble into the region of the gold mines. The road to Knoxville lay through the section of country still mostly inhabited by the Cherokee tribe of Indians, though it had been already surveyed and disposed of by lottery among the white inhabitants of the state. The portions of land actually cultivated by the Indians were, indeed, considered as their property, with whatever buildings they had erected. But as it was not the policy of the state to encourage their remaining, these also had been included in the lottery; so that each Indian's farm had a claimant ready to take possession of it as soon as the present owner should remove. Some years later, arrangements were made by which the Indians received compensation for their improvements, and consented to emigrate to the region provided for them beyond the Mississippi.

It was not until the second day after leaving Henderson, that Bryant forded the Chattahoochee, and entered the Indian country. He soon saw that it had already begun to be occupied by the more powerful race. He overtook a party, consisting of three families, who were, on their way to occupy the portions of land which had fallen to them in the lottery. They were travelling with large covered wagons, which served the purpose of tents for shelter when they rested at night. Only one family had slaves; and these, a woman and her boy, seemed to be on very familiar terms with their owners. Bryant had already observed a great difference, in this respect, between the slaves of small proprietors and the numerous servants on a large estate. Passing these, he travelled for some time in solitude. Then another river was to be forded, and on its opposite bank he found an Indian village. It was composed mostly of simple huts, resembling the log-cabins of the border settlers; but among them were some houses of commodious size and neat appearance; and the brown faces that appeared at the doors and windows of some among them showed that these also were dwellings of the Cherokees. The men whom Bryant saw were clothed partly like their white neighbors; but the leggings of deer-skin, and the blanket worn instead of a coat, were marks of a different race. The heads of both males and females were generally uncovered, the blanket serving for a hood, in case such protection was needed. A few men, however, were seen dressed entirely in the manner of the whites; and on the other hand, Bryant met afterwards an Indian adorned with feathers and wampum, in the true aboriginal style. In the centre of the village was a neat building, which answered the purpose of church and court-house, combined. Our traveller made no stay in this village, as he had been directed to the home of a friendly chief, some miles farther on.

It was towards evening that he came upon a group of persons evidently returning from a successful day's hunting. A man and boy, in the common clothing of working people among the whites, were carrying quantities of birds, hares, and squirrels, while two negroes followed, bearing each a rifle over one shoulder, while over the other was the end of a stake, held horizontally between them, and supporting the carcass of a deer. Bryant had heard already that slavery had been adopted by the Indians from their white neighbors.

The party stopped on seeing the traveller, and he thought the looks of the older Indian betokened little pleasure in meeting a white man in the midst of his hunting-grounds. Bryant saluted him courteously, and inquired if there was any place near, where he could find provision for himself and his horse.

"None here but Indian," said the man, gruffly. "When white man come to Indian country, he take care of himself; he camp out. No expect Indian take care of him."

"But I do expect the Indians to take care of me tonight," said Bryant, good-naturedly; "for I have been travelling a long way, and must go a long way farther, before I get out of your country."

"You go across, den? May be you come to look out your lot?"

"No; I am going across to Tennessee. I came from Henderson, and Colonel Freeman told me I could find accommodations with John Coombs, a chief man among your people."

"Colonel Freeman send you? Colonel Freeman good man. I John Coombs, and if colonel send you, all right. Come along wid me."

Bryant followed this guide, of a race he had never seen till that day, going back over a portion of the road he had passed. The chief had the copper color, the straight black hair, high but receding forehead, and prominent cheek bones, which he had often seen in pictures of Indians. His questions, as they walked, showed that he still regarded Bryant with some suspicion; but by degrees this cleared away, and but for the slight imperfection of his English, his visitor might have thought himself still in the company of the cordial and intelligent circle from whom he had recently parted.

At length they reached a point in the road from which an opening through the trees disclosed a clearing, with a neat house, of two stories, built in southern fashion, its broad piazzas covered by the advancing roof, and its chimneys projecting at the sides. Bryant wondered that he had not seen this dwelling as he passed before; but a look in the opposite direction recalled to his memory how his attention had been then engrossed by the lovely scenery that opened to his view, where the woods, partially cleared for Coombs's plantation, had allowed the eye to rest on the north-eastern mountains.

Entering the house, he found it furnished in the same style with the better class of country dwellings in the regions through which he had passed, even to the luxury of a piano, upon which the daughter of his host played the popular songs, for the gratification of her father's guest. When she was gone, Bryant could not but express his pleasure and surprise.

"Yes," replied the mother, sadly; "she is too fine a girl to be sent off among the wild Indians out in the West."

In the evening, his host, learning from Bryant that he was from a different section of the country, entered into the history of the recent events relating to his tribe. He told of the progress they had made in the arts of life, of their adoption of a regular republican form of government, and of the increased desire, on the part of their white neighbors, for their removal on that very account, as they did not wish to have within their state limits a permanent population of a different race, and exercising independent authority. He told how near the state had come to actual collision with the United States upon the subject, and how, subsequently, the discovery of gold in the Indian country had brought in upon them crowds of adventurers. Bryant had been assured by Judge Hendrick and Colonel Freeman, that it was, in part, to guard the Indians from these intruders that the legislature of the state had prohibited, for a time, the residence of any white man among them. His host now told, with deep emotion, how the missionaries, whom they regarded as their greatest benefactors, had, in their zeal for the good of their converts, violated the provisions of this law, and were at that very time enduring imprisonment in the state penitentiary; and he owned that the necessity was becoming more and more apparent for the remnant of their people to emigrate to the West. Bryant recognized in the account a new version of the same tale which the history of the older states discloses — that the Indian race recedes before the advancing Saxon with such sad fatality, that even improvement on the humbler side, and the endeavor to do justice on the other, seem almost to hasten the ruin they should delay.

The evening meal was followed by the evening prayer, for none are more zealous than recent converts in the externals of religion; and the patience of the Cherokees in after years, when their wilder neighbors, the Creeks, flew to arms, showed that their conversion had not been to external forms alone. In the morning, after a plentiful repast, the traveller felt some doubt whether it would be proper to offer to his host — a man of distinction among his people — any payment for the refreshment he had supplied. He made the tender, however, and was glad to find it accepted; for in a thinly-settled country the traveller might fare ill if he were not at liberty to ask for food and lodging at any house; and he can only feel this liberty upon the understanding that compensation will be received.

After leaving the house of the friendly Indian, Bryant pursued his way through woods, interrupted at rare intervals by clearings. At times he stopped, to buy at some cabin the simple refreshment it might be able to supply. Towards evening, he judged, from the knowledge of distances which he had obtained, that he was near the boundary of Tennessee, if he had not already crossed it; and he began to hope that he soon should see some cottage where he might pass the night.

While these thoughts were in his mind, a turn of the road brought him in sight of a group of men equipped as soldiers, except that they were not in uniform. Some were seated or stretched at length on the ground; others were leaning on their muskets, or slowly walking while they talked with each other. At the sight of Bryant, the attention of all was fixed upon him; and while some loudly called to him to halt, they handled their arms in a manner which showed they were prepared to enforce their order. Bryant wonderingly obeyed, and, as they approached, inquired of the foremost by what authority they stopped a passenger upon the highway.

"By the authority of the State of Georgia," said the leader. "I am captain of the Georgia Guard; and our orders are to keep suspicious persons from entering the Indian country."

"But I am leaving it, not entering it," replied Bryant; "so, whether a suspicious person or not, your orders cannot apply to me."

"I shall judge of that myself," said the officer, consequentially. "If a man has been doing mischief in the Indian country, I shall see that he does not leave it very easily. Where are you from, and where are you going?"

"I am last from the camp-meeting at Henderson, and I am travelling to Knoxville."

"Are you a preacher?" said the man, with a contemptuous laugh. "You don't look much like one; but if you are, we've had enough of preachers in the Indian country, stirring up the red-skins to rebellion. Where did you sleep last night?"

"I am not a preacher, and I slept at Mr. Coombs's."

"*Mister* Coombs! John Coombs, the old red-skin, called Mister! Well, friend, go on; you're giving a pretty good account of yourself! Come all this way from a camp-meeting, but not a preacher; spent last night at an Indian's, and talk about him as if he was a gentleman! Let's hear some more, now. Do you live at Knoxville, or at Henderson?"

"Where I live is none of your business," replied

Bryant, indignantly. "I am travelling on my own affairs, and simply passing through the country which you are pretending to guard. In half an hour I should be out of it, if I am not in fact through it already."

"Whether you're through it or not makes no difference. A man can't come it over me about being on the wrong side of a line drawn through the woods, as I told that crazy fellow the other day. I reckon we must take you to keep company with him at the guard-house. Your answers are not satisfactory, young man, and you must just dismount and be searched."

Bryant saw that it was in vain to resist, and to save the indignity of a search, produced what he had about him. When he saw his pocket-book opened by the officer, he fully expected that it would be lightened of some of its bank notes. His suspicion wronged the man, however, for he was only doing what he supposed to be his duty, though in a pompous and ungracious manner. He looked at the money, evidently with some surprise at its amount, and then examined the miscellaneous papers which the book contained. Some "Notes in the case of Maxwell versus Allen," and some "Verses to a Loved One far away," were but slightly looked at. The receipts attracted more notice; the officer spoke with one of his men, and pointed to him the date of "Boston." But what confirmed their suspicions fully was a piece of paper, which, having once been wet through with the rain, had been carefully dried, and placed in the inmost fold of the pocket-book. It was Lizzie's note to her lover on the evening of the mob. The officer made out the faded pencil-marks with some difficulty, but on reading them, exclaimed, —

"'Crowd of people surrounding the house,' 'abolitionist!' 'escape!' This tells the story. You've just got away from being lynched; and I reckon you deserved it. I arrest you as a suspicious character, and shall detain you till I receive instructions from his excellency the governor."

Much to his vexation, our traveller found himself obliged to accompany his new acquaintances to the cabin they occupied as a guard-house. It was of logs, having a chimney built of slabs and plastered inside with clay, and was furnished with an unglazed window in front. Other similar huts were near, for the accommodation of the soldiers. A sentinel was before the door; and seated on the step was a man of middle age, whose appearance in such a scene struck Bryant with some surprise. His dress, though bearing marks of rough living, was such as indicated the gentleman, fashioned with that attention to comfort more than show that is rather English than American. His face showed boldness, intelligence, and humor. He was talking familiarly with the sentinel; and if he was a prisoner, one might judge that he was one who could relieve the tediousness of his confinement by a lively temperament and a playful fancy.

"Here comes our illustrious captain," said he, as the party drew near; "and by all that is valiant, he has taken another prisoner. I welcome you, sir, to my hitherto solitary cell."

"Sentinel," said the captain, "do you not know it is against my orders for you to have any talk with your prisoner?"

"Beg pardon, cap'n," said the man, trying to smother a laugh; "but he's so droll."

"Be not indignant, most valiant captain," said the man upon the door-step. "I must speak to you in Ercles' vein, for that alone suits one so great as you. I consider you the greatest man I ever saw."

"I cannot allow such remarks," said the officer, holding his head somewhat higher, however, and not ill pleased at the sarcastic flattery. He continued, "You will have a companion in the guard-house, sir. This man, like yourself, has been stopped under suspicious circumstances, and will be detained until we receive further orders."

"And when will your further orders arrive, most excellent captain?" said the gentleman. "Here have I, for three days already, played the part of a captive Conrad, or a prisoner of Chillon, to quote my old acquaintance, Lord Byron——"

"We shall hear to-morrow. I have reported to the governor, and I have no doubt he will order you to be sent to him at Milledgeville for examination."

"And you look to be either earl or duke, for catching me, as Jack Falstaff did for killing Percy! But no dignity, captain, could possibly increase your greatness."

The officer made no answer to this compliment, but having posted another sentinel, left the two prisoners to make acquaintance with each other. The first occupant of the guard-house courteously shared with Bryant such means of comfort as the place afforded; and a soldier soon appeared, bringing their evening meal. The salt pork and bread, and the tin cups of coffee, were not unacceptable; and after they had supped, Bryant inquired of his new companion how he had fallen into the hands of the guard.

"By my own wandering disposition," he answered; "a disposition that has led me into all sorts of places since I left my father's school-house in Berry Street, Boston. It has carried me to half the capitals of Europe, and now it has made me prisoner to this redoubtable Captain Bobadil of the Georgia Guard. I have been travelling in the West, from Ohio to Tennessee, collecting subscribers for my new magazine; and I must needs come into this Indian country, to see what sort of beings the aborigines made when they were half civilized. I thought I might make a story, or a play, or an article out of it; and true enough, I have made one, with myself and Captain Bobadil for the heroes."

"I agree with you that the pomposity of the captain is rather diverting."

"The greatest man I ever saw,—actually the greatest.

I have seen George the Fourth; and his brother, the present king; and Napoleon the Great; and old Louis le Désiré; and ever so many others; but the majesty of this man goes beyond them all."

At this moment the sentinel before their open door commenced singing. Bryant was beginning to speak, but his companion signed to him to be silent. He listened with a smile as if of pleasure; then suddenly tears came into his eyes. Bryant looked on him with surprise, for the melody and words, though beautiful, were familiar; they were sung all over the country; for it was "Sweet Home."

"Ah," thought the young man, "he is thinking of a sweet home of his own, to which this dreary place is a sad contrast." But he did not penetrate the depth of his fellow-prisoner's feeling.

As the strain ended, the man who had been so moved by it asked the sentinel, "Do you know who wrote those lines?"

"No," said the man, betrayed, by the suddenness of the question, into forgetfulness of the rule against conversing with those under guard.

"I did," rejoined the prisoner. The sentinel looked surprised and respectful; but he had by this time remembered his orders, and in silence resumed his walk.

"You wrote them!" said Bryant. "Is it possible? Are you then Mr. John Howard Payne?"

"You have heard of me then?" said the poet. "Hearing that man sing, brought back the memory of former days so strongly that it almost unmanned me. I have written about home, and where have I a home now?"

"The author of 'Brutus,' the author of those lines, must have a home in every American heart."

"Thank you for saying so," replied Payne; "but this does not look like it. But come; as it is growing cold, let us shut that window and door. There is something to answer for a fireplace here; and I have a box of the new invented matches, that kindle by rubbing. So we will sit together on these blocks, and talk over our past adventures. How is it that you came into the hands of the Philistines? Have you been stirring up the Indians, or meddling with the blacks?"

Bryant gave an outline of his story; and then, at his request, the poet related some of the incidents in his own life, from those early days when he marshalled the boys of his father's school in mimicry of war, or won their plaudits by his declamation, to his precocious appearance as author and actor; thence through his experience in connection with the stage, and as consul for the United States in a foreign port. At length the varied tale was ended. They lay down upon the heap of straw which covered the rough floor in one corner of the guard-house. Bryant's dreams led him far away from the wild region and the rude and suspicious men around him. He stood again with Lizzie beneath the honeysuckle at the window of that "sweet home" in Irvine. Again she looked upon him with features kindled by elevated thought, as when she repeated to him those lines of Lovelace. It was a stanza of the same poet that she whispered now: —

> "Stone walls do not a prison make,
>   Nor iron bars a cage;
> Minds innocent and quiet take
>   That for a hermitage.
> If I have freedom in my love,
>   And in my soul am free,
> Angels alone, that soar above,
>   Enjoy such liberty."

In the course of the next morning a messenger arrived, bearing a letter to the captain of the Guard. It contained a severe reprimand for the detention of Mr. Payne, with an order for his immediate release, and that of any other persons detained under similar circumstances. The travellers, taking leave of the crestfallen captain, proceeded to Knoxville, where Payne published an account of his imprisonment, which was read throughout the land, and occasioned no little excitement. The executive of Tennessee began to make inquiries whether the outrage had not been committed within the limits of that state; and from Georgia courteous invitations were sent to the author of "Home, Sweet Home." The Georgia Guard was immediately disbanded. As for Bryant's arrest, it was forgotten in that of his more distinguished companion; and it would not have been known, but for this veracious record, that John Howard Payne had had any one to share his confinement.

CHAPTER XX.

INTO THE LION'S MOUTH.

SOME three months after the occurrences recorded in our last chapter, a merchant vessel from New York lay outside the bar at Charleston harbor. It was near evening, but in the glow of the west the city could be seen beyond the level bay, amid the circuit of land scarce less level — the city, twelve miles off, its roofs and less prominent towers clustering round St. Michael's spire, which seemed the gigantic guardian of the whole. Thus had the vessel lain since morning; and now, while the other passengers awaited its delayed motion with a composure that seemed indifference, one gentleman exhibited signs of impatience and vexation. He walked the deck rapidly, stopping, however, frequently, to look towards the city, or to observe the motion of the few clouds, as if to gather from them some augury of possible progress. At length he approached the captain, who, standing by the side of the vessel, was looking also towards the distant city.

"No hope of getting there to-night, then, captain?" he inquired.

"No, Mr. Bryant, no hope, so long as wind and tide are against us this way. You see we need a high tide to take us across the bar, and when the tide has been high, the wind has been dead ahead. We may have to lay here four and twenty hours, or more."

"And the cars for Hamburg leave Charleston at seven to-morrow morning! Captain, I am on business of life and death — life and death! too truly," said he, interrupting himself. "I must leave Charleston for the interior to-morrow at seven. Now, is there any possible way that, for love or money, I can be taken up to the city to-night?"

"We might hail a fishing-boat, and see if the man would take you in," said the captain. "There are plenty of these negro fishermen returning to land about this time."

Bryant eagerly caught at the proposal, and before long a boat was seen and hailed; the bargain was struck, and Bryant, with his baggage, took his seat in the boat, with its dark oarsman, bade farewell to the captain and his fellow-passengers, and was on his way across the waters, then so peaceful and lonely, — since then the scene of such fierce and fatal conflict.

When the negro had rowed for some distance, crossing the bar which had proved such an obstacle to the entrance of the larger vessel, Bryant discovered himself to be nearing a bastioned fortress on his right, and learned that it was Fort Moultrie, of revolutionary memory.

The low shore on the left was not crowned by any military work; and Fort Sumter, in our day so famous, did not then occupy its wave-washed island in the central space.

The negro sung, as he rowed, a strange, wild strain, to such words as these. They might be entitled —

THE FISH AND THE FISHER-BOY.

"Take de bait, take de hook;
  Come along, brudder fish;
Don't you want to see de cook?
  Don't you want to see de dish?
First-rate cook, Dinah!
  First-rate dish she got!
O, you'll be happy dere
  Cooked smokin' hot!

"Take de hook, take de line;
  Come along, nigger boy;
Get your massa fish to dine;
  Dat's a sight to gib you joy!
First-rate man, massa,
  First-rate at a treat;
O, you'll be happy dere
  Seein' massa eat!"

Bryant laughed as he heard the sarcasm of the second verse. It was a sudden laugh, that seemed broken off by some thought that forbade it. Remembering how his incautious conversation with Toussaint had resulted, he made no comment to the negro on his song.

Darkness fell around them, and the stars came out,

while the city revealed itself across the waters by its lights, streaking the waves with reflected radiance. Bryant was more inclined to converse with himself than with his companion.

"I wonder," said he, inwardly, "whether this fort I have just passed will ever give forth war's thunder again. All is peace now; and it does not seem likely that any nation will care to disturb us, powerful as we are; and here, on this continent, remote from their centres of power, we can scarcely disturb them.

"But internal convulsions? Is there not trouble brewing with these Nullifiers? They talk desperately, but it can hardly be carried out. This state will not act alone, and no other state is wild enough to act with her. If they should,—I did not vote for Jackson, but he is at least a man. He will not let the Union go without a struggle.

"These fish! My oarsman rests his oars to pull one in that has caught at one of the lines he had fastened to the sides of the boat. There, die, poor creature, seized by rapacious man! When philanthropy has done away with war, will it take up the cause of such victims as you?

"What shall we reason? That philanthropy is wrong? No; but we must keep in view common sense, and the evident will of God. I will not interfere for the fish then; nor will I meddle with the fisherman, and turn his harmless sarcasm into burning anger at the injustice which his race endures.

"No, 'Sunny South'! your great evil is beyond my mending. But O, how it pervades with its influence all your life! Well, I may not interfere with others, but I and mine will be clear of it. Never have I regretted, in all that it has cost me, that I refused to defile myself with Witham's ill-gotten gold.

"Ah, that recalls my errand — my errand, which the only friend who knows of it calls insane. Well, I have counted the cost, and I will not shrink, though it be from death. The father must be saved, wretch as he is, for truth's sake, and for his daughter's.

"His daughter's! Can she ever be mine? Not only a slave-dealer's, but a murderer's daughter? For he intended to murder, though not the man he killed; and if law had its strict course, the intention and the deed, both complete, though applied to different objects, would make him fully guilty of the crime of murder.

"Does honor bid me give her up for that? She will say so; I say differently. True honor bids me stand up for the innocent and the unfortunate. But down, idle hopes! My own life is in more danger than his. Well, let me do my part bravely; and if I fall, the victim of another riot, I fall without real dishonor, if I fall without guilt."

And now, the island of Castle Pinckney passed, the boat reached the wharf in the rear of the Exchange; and having paid his sable convoy, Bryant called a porter, and found his way to Jones's Hotel.

In the parlor, at Jones's, an elderly gentleman and lady were standing, habited as just returned from some evening engagement. They had been accompanied back to the hotel by others, who were now taking leave of them with expressions of courtesy.

"I am sorry," said a gentleman, "that your stay in Charleston is so short, Mr. Livingston, that we have not time to see more of you, and to show you what is worth seeing in our city."

"We should be delighted to stay longer among such hospitable friends," he replied, "but the business that brings us south is too pressing for delay, and indeed makes us too anxious to allow much thought for any thing else. But if all turns out well, we shall have a fund of agreeable recollections to dwell upon in future."

"I shall want to describe to my friends at the North," said Mrs. Livingston, "those beautiful churches. I hardly know which to admire most. St. Michael's is the finest building, but that venerable St. Philip's, with its walls and pillars so encrusted with marble monuments, is different from any thing I have seen elsewhere in our country."

"Then your accomplished sculptor," said Mr. Livingston, "Colonel Cogdell's name should be mentioned with Allston's, whom we claim by adoption, to show what South Carolina can do in the arts."

"While our friends in Orange Street show what she can do in poetry," added his wife.

"If you could stay over to-morrow, I should like to have you visit our citadel," said their southern friend; "the large, square building we passed on our ride this morning."

"A citadel!" said Mr. Livingston; "I heard the word used this morning, and was struck with it as something new in our country. What is it used for?"

"O, you know our peculiar population. They need some exhibition of military force to keep them in order. Our police, you may have observed, is military, with guard house and beat of drum; and the building I spoke of belongs to the state, but is garrisoned by United States troops."

"They are to leave soon, however," said another gentleman. "The governor has demanded back the citadel, and the requisition is to be complied with. But we must not keep our friends standing, Mr. Henderson." And with mutual good wishes, the Southerners departed.

"Ah," said Mr. Livingston, when they were gone, "that citadel and that military array tell volumes of the dangers as well as the evils, of the slave system. Strange, that men as intelligent and really noble as these should be the supporters of such a state of things."

"Did you observe," said his wife, "his anxiety when you were speaking with that poor fellow in the prison?"

"What, the one confined on a charge of circulating abolition documents? Yes; he seemed to think my simple questions of humanity would involve me as an accomplice. But, Lucy, did you notice the pillory, stored up in the court-house building? Who would have thought to see such a relic of the dark ages!"

They paused to listen to the sweet chime of St. Michael's bells. While they were yet ringing, the door opened, and Frederick Bryant was shown into the room.

"Ah, Frederick!" said Mr. Livingston, "then you have held firm to your purpose of coming south once more, though the last time so nearly cost you your life. Did not you think the old folks could be trusted to take care of their stray bird, but you must be coming after them?"

"No, sir; but my heart lay this way, and my duty too. But when did you arrive, and by what route, to get here before me?"

"We came by the new line of steamers between Charleston and Norfolk. They make a very easy passage, only stopping for wood and water at Cape Fear. I hear they talk of soon having a line direct to New York."

"O, before long there will be steamers to Liverpool," said Bryant. "You go on to-morrow, I suppose, as the trial is so near?"

"Yes; and we should have gone to-day, but we had friends here who were not to be denied. I have letters, too, since I saw you, that have relieved our anxiety in part."

"Letters from Lizzie?"

"From Lizzie and from Judge Hendrick. He has been all kindness. He and Mrs. Hendrick would have had Lizzie stay at their house, if she had been willing; but the noble girl would not leave Mrs. Witham, borne down with sorrow, and in declining health; and so, ever since Witham's arrest, they have boarded together at a house near the jail. There was a little left from the wreck of his property, which suffices for the present."

"The wreck of his property!" said Bryant.

"Had you not heard that nearly all he had was lost at a blow, by the failure of the Bank at Xenophon? The failure was entire. Nothing could be found to explain where the funds had gone; and no possibility, it seems, of calling any one to account in a legal manner. One of the losers, however, took the law into his own hands, by shooting the president of the bank in open day; and such was the public feeling, that at last accounts he had not been arrested for it."

"It has gone then," said Bryant; "gained by the crimes of its possessor, lost by the crimes of others! There passed away the obstacle that once was all that stood between Lizzie and me. But O, what obstacles there are now!"

"By what I hear from Lizzie," said Mr. Livingston, "her father's comment on the loss was much like what you have just made. He seems to be a changed man. He declares that he did not intend to kill Smith; but the pistol was found in his hand, hot from its recent discharge, and Smith dead on the ground before him. It is known that he had a quarrel with Smith, and had turned him out of the house, and that high words had passed between them since; so no one there believes him but his daughter. I confess, I doubt his story myself, for he gives no explanation why he fired the pistol; and he seems to feel as one who has the stain of blood on his soul. The Methodist minister who attends him says he should think him a true penitent, if he would but confess."

Bryant made no answer, but stood with contracted brows, as in deep and painful thought. Mr. Livingston continued:—

"Some have fancied that he fired in your defence; but that does not agree with other facts, for the story is, that you were hustled out of the way among the students just after the people in the house locked the door; that you ran round to the stable, and took the first horse you found, which happened to belong to Judge Hendrick. They were beginning to call you hard names for it, but Judge Hendrick silenced them, by declaring that you had sent back the horse, and paid handsomely for its use."

"Which he would not receive, however," said Bryant. "He handed the money I sent to the treasurer of the Orphan Asylum, from whom I received a note of thanks, accordingly. Well, they are ingenious in accounting for my disappearance. Let it pass for true till I tell the story myself."

"But are you crazy enough, Frederick, to venture in among those wild beasts again?" Mrs. Livingston spoke with deep concern. "If your testimony on the trial is of importance, can you not as well write your statement, and send it from here?"

"Yes," said Mr. Livingston; "have your deposition taken before a magistrate."

"I have thought of that," said Frederick. "It might possibly answer; but in such a matter as this, an error might cost life — the life of Lizzie's father. If I merely sent my statement, though sworn to, they think so hardly of abolitionists, that, supposing me to be one, they would suspect me of falsehood and perjury. There would be no opportunity for cross-examination, and the counsel opposed would take their revenge for this by dwelling on the improbability of my statement. Besides, it seems to me, the most straightforward, manly way is, to go right there, and tell my own story."

"And the most straightforward, manly way, you will do to a certainty," said Mr. Livingston. "But have you no news yourself, Fred?"

"None as late as yours, sir. My voyage has been a long one. I hoped, when I sailed from New York, to have been in Tusculum a week ago; but I should not even have been here to-night, but that I hired a negro to bring me up to the city in a boat. The ship is courting the obstinate breezes out there, beyond the bar."

"But you had letters before you left."

"From Judge Hendrick, as I told you, and from young Edward Elmsley, in reply to one of thanks, and excusing my desertion of him in the scuffle, which I never have felt quite easy about. He forgives me, however, and makes light of the bruises he received; but he writes that he should like to catch a real abolitionist, and help to do him up in soft cotton. Then I have one from Lizzie, sad as sad can be. It was written before the change you speak of had come over her father, or at least before she was fully aware of it. Her religious faith alone seems to sustain her."

"That change must strengthen her greatly. Yet there is enough of trial in the case," said Mrs. Livingston, "to make us very sad for our poor girl — her father in danger of his life on a charge of murder, and, at the best, a ruined man; her step-mother failing; and herself compelled to hush every sorrow of her own in order to minister to others."

"That necessity perhaps may be a blessing," said Mr. Livingston. "Her own burden may be less felt in her efforts to help those around her to sustain theirs."

"But, my dear, she thinks of them too much. That low-bred, quarrelsome man, and that vulgar woman! If they get out of this trouble safe, what comfort can Lizzie ever have in living with them? O, she *must* come and stay with us again; she ought not to refuse, and she must not."

"Do you think, then," said Bryant, "there is any

hope of her consenting to it? I have been afraid not, she seemed so devoted to what she considers her duty. And I love her all the better for it, too."

"I don't know; we must try. What time must we leave to-morrow, Mr. Livingston?"

"At seven o'clock, they say. And after all the fatigue you have had to-day, you had better rest now, to be ready for an early start in the morning."

CHAPTER XXI.

THE TRIAL.

THE trial of John Witham for the murder of Daniel Smith was to take place at Johnsonville; for Tusculum, though the seat of a college, did not join to that honor the dignity of being the county town. The case had excited no slight amount of attention, as the accused and his victim were both well known in the vicinity, and as popular report connected the occurrence with the absorbing topic of abolition, and the always interesting theme of love. It was generally agreed that Smith had been a suitor for Witham's daughter; most people said, an accepted suitor, until the arrival of the young Northerner had induced the intended bride to treat her lover with coldness. This, joined with his patriotic feelings, had led him to unmask and attempt to punish the abolition agent; and hence, it was said, had arisen the fatal quarrel. There were some, indeed, who maintained that the Yankee was the murderer; and more would have willingly believed this, but that Witham's language implied an admission of the act, though not of the intention, and that the pistol found in his hand gave testimony too clear for them to doubt. Much was the subject disputed among the crowd assembled in the Johnsonville tavern; and many were the bets made respecting the result of the trial, over glasses of mint-julep.

We will not pause there, but enter the court-house, where persons known to us are already assembled. Judge Hendrick having to appear as a witness, his place of dignity is filled by another. Mrs. Witham is too ill to be near her husband; but Lizzie is there, though looking pale and worn. Mrs. Livingston is seated next; and at her side is her husband, with his gray hair and his benevolent though energetic countenance. Bryant would have accompanied them; but such strong representations were made of the danger, not only to himself, but to others, of his being known to be present, that he had yielded, and stood undistinguished among the spectators. His friend, Mr. Stevens, of Royalton, occupied a seat near the Livingstons.

Lizzie sat with her eyes cast down, conscious of the gaze of the crowd; but her look was not one of unmingled sorrow or fear. From the expression of her father's features at the last glance she had ventured to take, she had said to herself, "Ah, if man condemns himself, I believe that he has found forgiveness elsewhere." Never had she loved him so much as now, when she sat by his side to witness his trial for a deadly crime; and yet, in her thankfulness for his repentance, the agony of suspense as to his fate was almost unfelt.

And the old, loved friends of her childhood were near. They had travelled, in their age, the long journey to be with her now. She had wept, last night, on that kind, maternal breast; she had given a daughter's kiss to her revered protector. That they were there, was joy in itself; and it was deepened when she thought that now her father was brought near to them by religious faith and hope. More than ever before, her complicated filial duties and feelings seemed to be in harmony.

There was another: did she look at him? They had had an interview yesterday, its tenderness rendered solemn by the terrible crisis at which they stood. Now, she knew he was near; her cautious glance had found him. Would he be safe, would he be prudent, so near the scene of his former danger?

The shock which came to Witham, when he found himself stained with the blood of an unexpected victim, among its other effects upon his character, had made him more tender of his daughter's feelings and reputation. At first, he had been too much overcome by horror at the deed he had committed, to say to those who questioned him, that he had aimed the pistol at Bryant; and this forbearance, at that time accidental, he had afterwards resolved to continue. He would not have his daughter know that he had sought the life of her lover; still less would he have her name mingled loosely, in public speech, with the details of a dreadful crime. As for Lizzie, she had shrunk within the window after her parting with Bryant, and had fainted at the confusion that ensued. She had been told afterwards that Smith had been shot by her father, and knew that the latter admitted the act, but represented it as unintentional. Engaged in attendance now upon her imprisoned father, and now on her sick step-mother, she had shrunk from hearing details of a revolting character, and was, therefore, little acquainted with the circumstances of the fatal deed.

Silence had been commanded, and the proceedings of the court commenced. There had been some difficulty in impanelling the jury, for few in the neighborhood had failed to express an opinion when their fellow-countryman, Smith, was shot by one who, though he had resided among them long, was still known to be an Englishman. But the difficulty was not increased by the prisoner challenging any without cause; and at length the jury was complete, the indictment was read, and the prisoner was called to answer, Guilty or Not Guilty.

"Guilty enough," replied Witham — "but not of what I am now charged with. It is true I killed Dan Smith ——"

"Enter a plea of Not Guilty, Mr. Clerk," said the judge, hastily. "The prisoner will be heard by his counsel, and by himself at the proper time. At present, he must keep silence."

The state's attorney now rose, and presented a statement of the case. He was a young and ambitious lawyer; and not doubting that he was bringing a murderer to deserved punishment, he thought rather of what arguments would have most effect upon the jury, than of what he could most legitimately employ. There was a motive which, whether the real one or not, he could impute to Witham with some show of probability, and which, if he could lead the jury to believe it, would prejudice them strongly against the prisoner: this was, a participation in the abolition views and purposes which had been charged on Bryant. He determined, therefore, to represent that Witham killed Smith in defence of the unpopular stranger, — the incendiary, — whom the just anger of the people sought to punish.

"Yes, your honor, and gentlemen of the jury," he continued, after having suggested this idea, "we are prepared to prove to you that this man, this agent of a nefarious association at the North, organized for the very purpose of spreading through our fair southern land insurrection, murder, and rapine in all their vilest forms, — that this man arrived at the prisoner's house on the morning of the day on which the murder was committed. We will prove, not merely that he had incautiously given hints of his fell designs, but that he had deliberately endeavored to excite a slave to become the leader of an insurrection. We will prove that, on his arrival at the hotel, the abolition agent endeavored at first to put off a meeting with his host until they could discuss their fell designs in private; that the prisoner, inadvertently, no doubt, defeated this purpose by recognizing his visitor; that he immediately endeavored to repair his error, and to lull suspicion, by a shallow pretence of unfriendliness towards the new comer; but that, when the sagacious, brave, and patriotic Smith, and the other gentlemen present, began to perceive and develop the character of the incendiary, he changed his course entirely, became the protector of the man against whom he had pretended hostility, and not only yielded him lodging, but received him into the most intimate connection with his own domestic circle. We could make this still more clear but for that provision of our laws which prevents the testimony of negroes from being taken in a court of justice. For once, let that provision, which, wise and just as it is, has been so maligned by abolitionists, extend an undeserved but magnanimous protection to the secret plottings of its enemies; we have still enough of evidence to show their guilty nature. We shall prove, by the evidence of many witnesses, that when the heroic Smith, indignant at the treacherous designs which he had unmasked, attempted to inflict personal chastisement on the incendiary, the prisoner gave his aid to that incendiary, and violently ejected the patriot from his house; we shall show that when a number of citizens, justly indignant, assembled to inflict condign punishment on the abolition agent, the prisoner, in a scornful and vindictive manner, refused to hear what their brave leader had to say regarding the object of their coming; that he locked the door of his house in the face of his incensed fellow-townsmen, taking under his protection the agent of insurrection and murder; for we shall prove to you, gentlemen, by the highest testimony, that the abolitionist Bryant was with the prisoner in the house. Circumstances combine to show that while this man was endeavoring to escape through the court, between the house and the negro quarters, he was intercepted by the gallant and watchful Smith. Here, apparently, a struggle took place: the base incendiary was on the point of being mastered by the chivalrous son of the South, when his protector, the prisoner now at the bar, raised a felon hand, and our state was deprived of one of her bravest sons.

"Gentlemen of the jury, I have completed thus the outline of the transaction, as we suppose it to have been. To constitute murder, the court will undoubtedly inform you, there must be the fatal act, and proof of the criminal intention. The act is not denied; and if it were, its proof would be easy, for the prisoner was found standing stupefied, the moment after he had fired the fatal shot, with his victim before him, and the pistol, still hot from its discharge, in his hand. The criminal intention is proved by the facts I have now related.

"But, before I proceed to the examination of witnesses, I will meet one objection, which will, undoubtedly, be urged against the view I have taken. My learned brother, the counsel for the defence, will probably prove to you that the prisoner at the bar has exercised the calling of a buyer and seller of negroes. He may spare himself the trouble of calling witnesses to prove the point; we admit it, and while we believe that the calling is alike legal and necessary, we do not think it one of that elevated character that speaks much in favor of him who sustains it. But my brother will probably ask you whether you think it credible that a negro-dealer should become the agent of abolitionists, and, by consequence, an abolitionist himself?

"And why not, gentlemen of the jury? If a man can, for the sake of sordid gold, subdue his natural feelings to an employment which, if lawful and necessary, is certainly repulsive, is it likely that those feelings are delicate enough to keep him from an unlawful employment, provided it is but profitable? We do not suppose that the abolitionists employ their nefarious agents at the South without price. The vast resources of the North are, in a great measure, at their command; and to engage an agent in the unsuspected guise of a dealer in slaves would give them an advantage well worth a heavy outlay. We can prove, too, that indications had been given, by the prisoner, of an alteration of feeling with regard to his occupation, and a purpose to exchange it for another. He is known, during the last spring, to have purchased a slave woman, with the avowed purpose of selling her in New Orleans, and subsequently to have abandoned that intention, and disposed of her to a neighbor of her former owner. Since that occurrence, he is believed to have made neither purchase nor sale. It is probable that this change was insisted on by the fanatical party to which he had sold himself.

"We will now, may it please your honor, attend to the examination of witnesses. When these have been heard, it will be for you, gentlemen of the jury, to vindicate, by your verdict, not only the violated law and the sacredness of human life, but peculiarly the safety of southern homes, and the permanence of southern institutions, while you inflict due punishment upon the murderer of one who bravely fell in their defence."

Murmurs of applause, and expressions of surprise and indignation, had passed through the crowd during the address of the state's attorney; but when he ended, these feelings, thus far held in check, burst forth in long and repeated plaudits, which the crier vainly endeavored to check. When these had nearly subsided, there mingled with them cries of rage against the prisoner. "Down with the murderer!" "Hang the abolitionist!" Such were the shouts; and the crowd pressed against the prisoner's dock, as if about to dispense with judge and jury. Lizzie trembled in every limb, but, rising, stood facing the crowd, leaning against the partition which separated her from her father. As she looked round on them, she saw Bryant's eye fixed upon her. His face was pale, but the lips firmly compressed. As she looked, he raised his hand, and pointed upwards; Lizzie sunk again to her seat, strengthened by the mute suggestion; and at the same moment the voice of the judge, sternly raised, restored order in the court.

"This disturbance must not be suffered," he said. "The officers of the court will arrest any person guilty of renewing it. The accused is entitled to a fair trial, and the law of the land will accord impartial justice."

The examination of the witnesses for the prosecution now commenced. The main facts of the death of Smith from a pistol shot, of the pistol being found in Witham's hand, of the previous expulsion of Smith from the house, and the high words which had passed in the presence of the mob, were easily established. The witnesses who proved them were, however, strictly cross-examined by the counsel for the defence, with regard to the position of the body, as indicating the attitude of the deceased at the time of receiving the mortal wound. As the cross-examination elicited the fact that Smith was shot while his face was turned from his assailant, proving that the deed was not done in self-defence, the state's attorney smiled, and looked significantly toward the jury.

Evidence was now introduced on the subject of Bryant's visit, and the commotion which resulted from it. This led to frequent objections from the counsel for the defence; but in most instances the objections were overruled by the court. Among the witnesses summoned was Judge Hendrick, who testified that he passed through the house to avoid the crowd; that on his way he saw both Witham and Bryant, but not together; and that he left the latter alone in the court-yard. The judge was not asked whether he had seen Bryant afterwards, not only as the question seemed unnecessary to the case, but because it was thought best not to inquire too closely into the mode of the young man's escape. For the same reason, and in deference to Judge Hendrick's character, the counsel for the defence declined entering upon any cross-examination.

Young Elmsley and some other of the students were examined, principally with regard to what had passed between Witham and Smith in the piazza. They testified that when the struggle was over, which had commenced with Smith's attack upon the stranger, neither Witham nor Bryant was to be found, and the door of the house was locked.

The presentation of the case on the part of the state was now completed, and the court awaited the argument of the counsel for the accused.

CHAPTER XXII.

THE DEFENCE.

THE lawyer who now rose to defend the prisoner was one of the most eminent men in his profession in the state. He was from Royalton, the residence of Mr. Stevens. How his services had been obtained or were to be compensated, Witham himself did not know; but at an early period after the charge was first made, he had called on the family, and had given to the prisoner's daughter a note of introduction from the Rev. Mr. Stevens, which procured for him the unrestricted management of the case. He now rose to address the jury; and there was a hush of expectation, for Colonel Henley was not often heard to speak in the courts of that portion of the state. In fact, he was not often heard any where. His retiring disposition inclined him rather to the less public part of the business of his profession; but whenever an occasion arose which called him forth, he was always found equal to it. He was one whom those honors sought in vain, which other men seek for. It was thought by his friends that his talents would have shone most brightly in a military capacity; and had the war of 1812 continued to another campaign, his rank of colonel would have been changed to that of brigadier-general. For some years from that time he had cultivated his more peaceful profession with assiduity and success, and had engaged to some degree in political strife; but a duel into which this had led him, though resulting bloodlessly, had occupied for a time the attention of the country, far and wide. He had been judged severely by some, and ridiculed by more. His proud heart shrunk within itself, and thenceforth he turned from politics, and, as far as he could, from public practice. Possessed of competence, and not ambitious to increase it, his appearance in the case now pending showed to those who knew him that he must be deeply interested in it, either from his love of justice or from personal feeling.

Colonel Henley's line of defence was marked out for him by the facts of the case, as he supposed them to be, and by what he knew of the temper of his southern fellow-citizens. After closely questioning Witham, he could not bring himself to believe the truth of the man's assertion, that he had not killed Smith intentionally; for the only alternative seemed to be that the pistol had gone off by accident, and the coincidence of this with the death of an enemy in a lonely place, was too improbable for him to yield it credence. Nor did he expect to make the jury believe it. But, though ill pleased with the prisoner's want of confidence in him, he resolved, if possible, to save his life.

He began, therefore, by remarking that his learned brother had needlessly connected with the case before them questions of a kind peculiarly suited to arouse the passions of their community. What had the killing of Smith to do with abolitionism? Only this: that the presence of an abolition agent, real or supposed, in the house, had been the cause or the pretence of that riot in which Smith lost his life. To suppose Witham himself an abolitionist was absurd — a man who had long lived in the country; who had not only held slaves, but traded in them; and who, if he was planning the destruction of those around him, must see his own family involved in the common ruin. Colonel Henley said that he yielded to none in his determination to allow no interference from abroad in southern institutions; but he thought it highly censurable to mingle that question, which so naturally stirred the southern blood, with the calm course of justice.

"The prisoner declares," said Colonel Henley, "that he did not design the death of Smith, at the time of firing the pistol. He does not declare that the pistol went off by accident. That it did is certainly possible; more probable, perhaps, that, though aimed and fired, the action was so involuntary as to leave no remembrance of design." Here a scornful laugh from the opposing counsel, and a look of incredulity from the judge, brought Colonel Henley to a sudden pause; and the proud blood mantled in his cheek as he sternly said that he thought a case on which the life of a human being depended no rightful theme of mirth. "But," he added, "allowing that there was intention, we trust to prove that there was cause sufficient to account for and to justify it.

"Here, gentlemen, was an assault made by this man Smith, and others, upon the dwelling of the prisoner. Turn your thoughts from the cause of the excitement, and regard for the present, as justice requires you to do, only the fact that a riot was going on, in which the prisoner's property and the very lives of himself and family were put in peril. Threats had been uttered by some, and in particular by Smith, of burning the house down, if the suspected person was not found. It will be brought in evidence to you, gentlemen, that when the prisoner was arrested, he had about him articles of value and business papers, such as men are not accustomed to carry on their persons: this fact shows the terror in which he had been placed, lest the threat of fire should be carried into effect. At the moment when his danger and excitement are at the highest, the man who had collected and inflamed the mob — the man who had threatened to fire his house — enters his enclosure, with the design, for aught that the prisoner knows, of carrying his threat into execution. I ask you, gentlemen, is there one of you who would not, under such circumstances, defend his home? Admit that the prisoner, in denying that he intended to kill Daniel Smith, is only exercising the right of every accused person not to give evidence against himself; admit that he did really intend it; I ask which of you would not have intended the same, when an enemy rushed into your premises to set your house on fire. Gentlemen, if this supposition is correct, all for which I can blame the prisoner is an excess of caution in not at once stating the truth, and throwing himself on your just sense of what is due from a husband and father to his endangered family; nay, of what every man, deserving of that name, will do by the very instinct of his nature, when he is assailed. Let him learn, gentlemen, from your verdict, that he has underrated the justice and generosity of your sentiments."

If one might judge from the thoughtful looks of the jury, and the profound silence of the whole assembly, a deep impression had been made by the appeal of the counsel for the defence. But the train of argument by which his legal protector sought to save him was far from being agreeable to Witham himself. Conscious of innocence with regard to any intention of taking the life of Smith, Witham felt as if his counsel was betraying his cause in admitting the thought of his having had such intention. At the moment, therefore, of that deep silence, he burst forth with the words, —

"I didn't mean to shoot Dan Smith. I fired at the abolitionist, at Mr. Bryant. I didn't want to tell this, for —— "

"Silence," exclaimed at once judge, crier, and counsel; but the words had been spoken, and had been heard by all. Colonel Henley struck his hands together in vexation. The state's attorney rose with an air of triumph.

"Gentlemen of the jury," he said, "the declaration which has just been made is worth your notice."

Colonel Henley interrupted him by protesting against such a declaration being received as evidence.

"I shall not," said the state's attorney, "contest the point which my learned brother has raised. I refer to that declaration not for the direct testimony it gives, for I presume no one here considers it as true; it is but the desperate expedient of a criminal to save his life. I share, gentlemen, your pity for the unfortunate man, as his condition is shown in these turnings and windings; but that pity must not prevent us from doing our duty. He has perceived, gentlemen, your just feeling against the incendiary abolitionist, and can any thing be more transparent than his effort to obtain your favor by pretending that his fatal shot was fired against that enemy of southern peace? For myself, gentlemen, I will believe his assertion when that man Bryant, who then succeeded in rescuing himself from the just punishment of his crime, shall venture back from the safety of his northern home, to stand in the circle of those from whom he then escaped, and tell us that the prisoner fired at him."

"He is here," cried a voice from among the spectators; and, coming forward, Frederick Bryant desired permission to give his testimony.

CHAPTER XXIII.

THE UNEXPECTED WITNESS.

THE surprise occasioned by the appearance of Bryant was evident all around. Counsel, prisoner, and jury started to their feet. Lizzie, though aware of his presence, had not till then seemed to realize the danger in which it placed him. She clasped her hands in agony, bent forward, and closed her eyes, as if to shut out the whole dreadful scene. Mr. and Mrs. Livingston looked on with trembling interest. Mr. Stevens came forward to meet his friend, shook him cordially by the hand, and introduced him to Colonel Henley.

"Who is this person?" inquired the judge, as order was restored. "Does the counsel for the defence desire to introduce him as a witness?"

"I do, may it please your honor," replied Colonel Henley. "This, gentlemen, is the person so frequently referred to, and, I cannot but hope, so unjustly characterized as the abolitionist Bryant. Whatever ground there may be, or may not be, for the prejudice against him, he has ventured himself here with a bravery which all must honor, to give his evidence in this important case, this case of life and death. He is here before a court of impartial legal justice, by whom he will be patiently heard, and from whom he will meet all just protection." He spoke with stern impressiveness, for there were marks of commencing tumult among those around.

The state's attorney started to his feet. "I share," said he, " please the court, in the general surprise at the appearance of this witness. I could have wished, for his own safety, and that the course of justice should not be disturbed by tumult, that he had not thought it necessary to venture again into a state which he had but recently found had little relish for his company. But since he is here, far be it from me to object to his being fully and fairly heard. He comes among us to give evidence in an important case, and no friend of justice and of our country can prevent him from bearing his testimony, or injure him for so doing. Let him speak freely then. I, for one, will protect him, if necessary, to the last drop of my blood, so long as he confines himself to the simple duty of a witness."

Bryant was accordingly sworn, and proceeded, in answer to the questions addressed to him, to give an account of what he knew in relation to the case. Those questions, however, were at times so general, that nearly all that had occurred during his stay in Tusculum was included. That he had known Witham and his daughter in that northern village where the latter had been adopted by the excellent pair who were now present; that he had come south on business with Witham which he declared on oath had nothing to do with any abolition designs, but was strictly private in its character; all this appeared, and the hearers, as they saw Lizzie's brightening look of hope and blush of modesty, drew their own conclusion as to the nature of that business. Ingenuously he related the conversation into which the peculiar name of the slave Toussaint had led him, injudiciously, as he admitted, but without a thought of instigating insurrection. He declined entering into the details of his interview with Witham, but testified that they had quarrelled; that he had entered the house from the piazza during the riot, not under Witham's protection, but that of another, whom he declined to name; and that while in the central court he had heard the report of a pistol, and had believed it to be aimed at himself.

The evidence was heard with deep attention. It was in a tone of surprise and respect that the state's attorney addressed the question, "What motive had you for coming hither, at the risk which you must have known, to give evidence in this case?"

"The motive of doing justice. This man was accused of the intentional murder of Smith. I knew that, as far as related to Smith, the occurrence was accidental."

"But the prisoner had intended to take your own life."

" That did not alter my obligation to tell the truth, when he was charged unjustly with taking the life of another."

" Had you no other — no softer motive in the case?" inquired the lawyer, with a meaning look.

" I admit that I had another motive. It was to protect an innocent wife and daughter from disgrace and misery. But neither this nor any of my private thoughts, which you may imagine, was necessary to bring me here. I am a lawyer, sir, as well as yourself, and I am vowed to the service of justice."

" I do not desire," said the state's attorney, " to prolong the cross-examination. I will but remark to the jury, before dismissing the witness, that his evidence, if admitted, is conclusive against the prisoner." A murmur of surprise passed round the court. " Yes," he resumed, " by the prisoner's own declaration, he intended murder — the murder of Mr. Bryant; Mr. Bryant's testimony confirms this. The deed of death, then, being done with intention, its guilt is not affected by the fact that it fell, through accident, upon the wrong victim. Death, — the death of an unoffending person, — for such Mr. Bryant's manly, straightforward narrative, and the courage of conscious innocence which has brought him here to tell it, declare him to be, — his death was the design; — death also was the result; the design and the result go together, and form the crime of deliberate murder."

As the state's attorney closed, the prisoner groaned

aloud, and covered his face with his hands; Lizzie sat pale and breathless. After a moment's pause, Bryant, who was still on the witness stand, begged permission to speak.

"It is due," said he, "to the prisoner, and to justice, that I should declare the cause of his hostility to me. In a case so solemn as this, where life is involved, I must speak of things which otherwise are held most private. I testify, therefore, that I came to the prisoner's house, to ask of him the hand of his daughter, whom I —— But that is nothing to the purpose. I had received his consent, and all seemed —— when a discussion arose between us on the subject of slavery. I testify here, — and I am prepared to meet whatever danger the declaration may place me in, — that I refused to become his son-in-law, if I was to be in any way involved in the guilt of his business as a slave-dealer, even by receiving any share of the property he had accumulated. We parted in anger. Afterwards, in making my escape from the house, he came upon me at the moment of a farewell interview with his daughter; and then, as I believe, not with malice prepense against myself or any one, but on sudden impulse, the fatal shot was fired. It can avail nothing, probably, to extenuate his act; yet I will say, that for that act, and for the anger that caused it, he has my free forgiveness."

Judge Hendrick now came forward, and desiring to be again heard as a witness, disclosed the part he had

had in Bryant's escape, confirming his statements with regard to the manner in which it had been effected.

When his evidence was finished, Colonel Henley approached Lizzie, and said a few words to her in a low voice. She started, and seemed to shudder, but bowed in acquiescence. The lawyer turned to the court, and said, "If any doubt remains as to the correctness of Mr. Bryant's statement, Miss Witham is prepared to give her evidence." With a pitying voice, the judge observed that her testimony certainly might be of great importance; and she was called to the witness stand. But as she rose, her agitation was such, that the judge directed that she should give her testimony where she was seated.

"I will make the examination as short as possible," said Colonel Henley. After the oath was administered, he continued, "Miss Witham, did you see Mr. Bryant on the evening of the riot?"

"I did, sir," she replied, in a voice low, but clear.

"Where were you at the time?"

"At the window of the building used as kitchen and negro quarters, where my father had placed us, as farthest from the mob."

"Please to relate what followed."

"I remember seeing my father, and how angry he looked, and that I thought Mr. Bryant was killed. I do not remember any thing else."

"That will do; I will ask you no further questions."

The state's attorney refrained from cross-examination. Mrs. Livingston whispered to Lizzie that she would leave the court with her; but the latter pointed to her father, and shook her head.

The charge of Judge Stanley to the jury instructed them in the distinctions between deliberate murder, manslaughter, and justifiable homicide. To the last he gave a latitude unknown to the jurisprudence of most other communities. He referred to a decision then recent, by which a man who shot down another in the street had been held guiltless, because the person he killed was known to have threatened his life. He spoke also of the charge given by an eminent western judge, holding that for deeds committed by a mob, no individual can be held accountable. The former of these decisions, he said, might lead the jury to consider how far, if the death of Smith was intended, the previous quarrel, and the riot in which he was engaged, would extenuate the offence. But if, on the other hand, the fatal shot was intended for Bryant, the jury might find reason for a favorable judgment on either of the two grounds, should the evidence appear sufficient to sanction them—that the deed was the act of sudden passion from domestic provocation, or that the prisoner joined in the feeling of the crowd. The citizens, he said, from a patriotic impulse, though in a disorderly manner, were pursuing a person thought to be an incendiary. "I do not myself believe," said he, "that this suspicion was correct: the deportment of the witness, Mr. Bryant, and the very fact of his appearing again among us with such modest fearlessness, vindicate him against the charge. Nor do I approve of lawless gatherings to punish supposed crime. But while our institutions remain as they are,— and who among us would wish them changed?— any rumor of interference from abroad will infallibly produce such gatherings. And when a crowd are assembled, and are seeking, with feelings we cannot entirely condemn, the punishment of one whom they consider guilty, the act of any one person in firing upon him must be considered as the act of the whole assembly; to be regretted, indeed, and blamed, but not to be visited with punishment. There were hundreds of persons assembled on that night, seeking the life of Mr. Bryant. In the eye of the law, all were equally guilty. It is not right to punish one for the crime of hundreds. The decision, then, of Judge L—— is applicable to this case; and the shot, if fired in the pursuit of a supposed abolitionist, must be considered as the act, not of the individual, but of the assembled multitude.

"But, gentlemen of the jury, crime must be punished, and the dignity of the law maintained. If you believe, therefore, that the prisoner fired that shot with deliberate malice against either Smith or Bryant,— that is, from any motive except recent provocation or patriotic impulse, — then it was murder, and you must find him guilty. I must remind you, however, that if there is any doubt in your minds, the prisoner is entitled to its benefit. With this, gentlemen, I leave you to the discharge of your great and responsible office."

The jury, without retiring from the room, rendered a verdict of "Not Guilty."

CHAPTER XXIV.

THE CONCLUSION.

THE announcement, which gave safety to the accused, was received by the crowd with a shout of applause. Compassion for the danger in which he was placed, admiration of his daughter's beauty and modesty, and respect for the courage of the young man who had ventured into the scene of his former danger to bear testimony in favor of one who had sought his life, — these mingled feelings influenced the better portion of the crowd. But there were others who could see in the result nothing but the escape of one abolition incendiary by the false oath of another. As the applause subsided, some of these gave vent to their anger in hisses; but the voice of the crier restored silence, the prisoner was pronounced acquitted, and the court dismissed. In a few moments, the spectators were crowding the passage from the hall, or standing before the court-house; some with congratulations to each other on the result of the trial; others with loud declarations, interlarded with many an oath, against the prisoner and the unexpected witness, whose testimony had been so important.

Within the court-house, deeper feelings found a more quiet expression. Witham himself, at the moment of hearing the verdict, had sunk down, covering his face with his hands. The work of repentance, begun within him by his own horror at the unexpected issue of his deed, and continued by the exhortations of the faithful Methodist minister, was now completed by the providential mercy that had rescued him from a felon's death. Thankful as he was, contrition was his deepest emotion. He felt himself to be a murderer in intention and in act, though the object of the intention and the victim of the act were different; and fresh from the acquittal of a human court, he breathed an earnest prayer for forgiveness before the bar of Heaven.

Lizzie had sunk fainting. She had nerved herself to bear sorrow, but was unprepared for joy. Her foster-mother bent over her, and called her by every endearing name; Bryant, assisted by his friend Stevens, had borne her near an open window, and laid her upon benches; he knelt by her side and chafed her hands, while Mrs. Livingston threw water upon her face. She opened her eyes at length, and looked around in a bewildered manner. Her father had joined the circle, and was bending over her. She looked up at him, and as she saw tears on his rugged cheeks, her own eyes filled; she folded her hands, and said faintly, "Thank God, my father is acquitted!"

"Acquitted! Yes, by man's court, but not by God's! I meant to commit murder — to murder you, Mr. Bryant;

you, so generous — Can you forgive me? If you can, perhaps God will forgive me too."

"I forgive you, Mr. Witham, with all my heart;" and the young man took the hand of the penitent in a cordial grasp. The Livingstons, and others who were around, followed his example.

"Now," said Mr. Livingston, "let us leave this place. Mr. Witham, we must have Lizzie for a while with us."

Lizzie was resting on Mrs. Livingston's breast, as she had done when a child; but at this she tried to rise, saying, "Thank you; but I must go back to my poor sick mother."

"Not now, Betsy," said Witham, in a more tender voice than she had ever heard from him. "Mother and I will both spare you now for a while. Go with your kind friends; but let us see you before night, that we may all thank God together."

Edward Elmsley now came forward, with a look of deeper concern than his words implied, for they were only an invitation to Mr. Bryant to dine at his father's, who resided a short distance from the town. Colonel Henley seconded the suggestion.

"You had better," said he, "be as much out of view as possible, not only for your own safety, but for the comfort of us all. Every right-feeling person approves your course; but all are not right-feeling in our part of the world, and I suppose not in any other."

Bryant hesitated, but Lizzie, too, pressed his going,

and with rather an ill grace, he accepted the proffered hospitality.

There were many persons standing around the courthouse door when the two came out. Elmsley's servant was holding the reins of a spirited horse, attached to a handsome specimen of those four-wheeled vehicles which, under the name of buggy, have nearly supplanted the old-fashioned chaise.

"Robert," said Elmsley, speaking louder than seemed necessary, "tell my uncle Burgess that I shall not be in to-day, as I said, because I have Mr. Bryant's company to dinner. You understand? I have Mr. Bryant's company to dinner."

He took the reins, and seated Bryant and himself. The young men both sat silent till they had turned into another street, when Elmsley exclaimed, —

"Now, Mr. Bryant, you think you are going to dine with me at my father's, a mile out of town; but you are mistaken. We are to dine at Petersville, twenty miles off; that is, if we have a chance to dine at all."

"What do you mean?" said Bryant, starting. "I am not ready to leave the place so soon."

"You don't want to make your exit from the end of a rope, I suppose? Nor even riding on a rail with a coat of tar and cotton? Ah, I have had a wish to see somebody tarred and cottoned, for the downy beauty of the thing."

"But, Mr. Elmsley," said Bryant, earnestly, "I cannot leave these friends without warning, and on a mere fancy of danger, without dishonor. If there is real danger, they are exposed to it, and ——"

"Not at all," said Elmsley. "Nobody would harm that old gentleman and lady, nor that young lady either, whom, I fancy, you are more anxious about. But listen. I know there is a plan to waylay you this evening, and punish you by Lynch law, on the old charge of abolitionism. I know it from the best of all reasons, because I was asked to join in it, by one that was not aware exactly how I stood towards you. Now, if you like the aforesaid tar and cotton, or riding on a rail, or forty stripes save one, or any other pleasant experience of that kind, I'll keep on to father's, and make old Dinah get us some dinner. She is the only person there to do the honors; for father, and mother, and William, and Mouse, are all dining at my uncle Burgess's. 'Mouse' is used, for shortness, for my sister Georgiana."

"But to desert my friends!" said Bryant.

"O, we'll take care of your friends. Much comfort it would be to them to have you caught."

"You are right," said Bryant, after a moment's pause, — not in their motion, however, for the horse went like the wind. "You are right; and I thank you with all my heart; but it is hard, it is galling, to be forced a second time to fly on this false and scandalous charge, and that at a moment when ——"

"Yes, when all seemed bright," said Elmsley; "I

understand you;" and there was a tone of sympathy in his voice that corresponded with his words. "But," he added, "you need not leave the state. Only remain away for a week or two; and you can either come back to Johnsonville, or arrange with your friends where else to meet them."

A ride of two hours, with Elmsley's noble horse, brought them to Petersville, where, after a hasty meal, they parted, Bryant taking the stage to Royalton, and Elmsley returning to Johnsonville. The lover, however, had found time to write a few lines to Mr. Livingston, excusing his desertion, and another letter, which renewed the offer of his hand and fortune to the daughter of John Witham.

"Say that you will be mine," he wrote, "and no danger, real or imagined, shall keep me from retracing the way to where I may claim you. If you still say no, it must be because it is right; and Heaven bless you; but it will be best for me not to see you again. Only, if any evil ever threatens you or yours, send but the slightest token, and you will see again before you your devoted friend, F. W. B."

Lizzie did not recall him to Johnsonville; for young Elmsley's information had been correct, as the occurrences of that evening proved. A number of men had left the hotel, where they had made no secret of their intention to try the abolitionist by Lynch law. They lingered around Rosemount — General Elmsley's house — till towards evening, when, instead of seeing any one issue from the gates, they saw the general's carriage approaching from the village. An explanation followed, and the plotters slunk away ashamed. The skill with which young Elmsley had baffled them, with the open approval of Bryant's course by the best men in the community, kept them quiet afterwards. Yet Lizzie and her friends thought it best not to expose her lover to a renewal of his danger.

But every other obstacle to their union was now removed. Her father had lost that ill-won property which Bryant had refused to touch; and he had gained that change of character which enabled him to begin life again, if in some humble occupation, yet in one which should not be felt as disgraceful by rightly-judging minds. His wife appeared so far improved in health by the issue of her husband's trial, that she combated the scruples on her account which Lizzie alleged. Mr. and Mrs. Livingston, though suppressing any urgent claim for their own pleasure, showed in all their demeanor how earnestly they desired to have again the company of their adopted daughter. Witham, though he had but recently found that union of true parental and filial feeling which could not exist while he was estranged from virtue, yet felt anxious to make up to his daughter for her past self-sacrifice. The advancing season seemed unpropitious for a journey north; but this objection was removed by

Mr. Livingston's proposing that himself and wife, with the young couple, should spend the winter in visiting other points of interest in the Southern States, and in the West India Islands.

It was the afternoon of a pleasant day in the early part of the mild southern winter, when the carriages of a bridal party stood before the door of Mr. Stevens's church, in Royalton. It was a humble building, but there was grace in its humility, as it stood among its trees, looking forth on the wide street that took its name from Greene, the friend of Washington, but which every visitor thought had been thus called from the verdure which, even at that season, held disputed possession with its trodden paths. From the first carriage descended the bridegroom and his friend, the minister; from the second, the bride, her father, and her adopted parents. Edward Elmsley followed, with Anna Stevens, sister of the clergyman, in the character of groomsman and bridesmaid. There were none besides; but the awe of a holy presence filled the house of prayer; and as the lovers spoke in subdued tones their mutual vows, all felt that they who had been true to duty when it forbade their union, would be faithful through life, where love and duty now combined to mark and to bless their course.

One marriage leads to another; and this young Elmsley found, from his casual association at that time with Anna Stevens. A warm friendship continued to unite them with those whose history had thus influenced their own. Another generation has now arisen; and for them the tree of slavery has borne the bitter fruit of civil strife. When the State of Georgia, influenced in part by feelings of mistaken honor, followed the rash leading of South Carolina, Frederick Bryant Elmsley entered the Confederate army, and is now — in 1864 — a captain in the Johnsonville Dragoons; while Edward Elmsley Bryant is major of the ——th Massachusetts Regiment. But the mothers of the young men, while engaged in works of charity for the poor, the sick, and the wounded of their respective sections, send thoughts of love beyond the lines of war. Mrs. Bryant thinks with pity of the sufferings of those among whom she once experienced generous protection; and Mrs. Elmsley does not forget her birthplace, and the home of her early years. Such memories are among the means that will establish a better harmony than ever in our land, when the great rebellion, and the barbarous system from which it sprung, shall alike have passed away.

HOME LIFE:

WHAT IT IS, AND WHAT IT NEEDS.

BY

JOHN F. W. WARE.

BOSTON:
WM. V. SPENCER.
134 WASHINGTON STREET.
1864.

www.ingramcontent.com/pod-product-compliance
Lightning Source LLC
Chambersburg PA
CBHW031745230426
43669CB00007B/498